Expectations, Rationality and Economic Performance

To my mother and the memory of my father

Expectations, Rationality and Economic Performance

Models and Experiments

Tobias F. Rötheli

Professor of Economics
University of Erfurt, Germany

Edward Elgar
Cheltenham, UK • Northampton, MA, USA

Published by
Edward Elgar Publishing Limited
Glensanda House
Montpellier Parade
Cheltenham
Glos GL50 1UA
UK

Edward Elgar Publishing, Inc.
William Pratt House
9 Dewey Court
Northampton
Massachusetts 01060
USA

A catalogue record for this book
is available from the British Library

Library of Congress Cataloguing in Publication Data
Rötheli, Tobias F.
    Expectations, rationality, and economic performance: models and experiments / Tobias F. Rötheli.
        p. cm.
    Includes bibliographical references (p.   ) and index.
    1. Rational expectations (Economic theory)—Mathematical models.
I. Title

    HB3731.R68 2007
    330.01'9—dc22   2006037095

ISBN 978 1 84542 742 9 (cased)

Printed and bound in Great Britain by MPG Books Ltd, Bodmin, Cornwall

Contents

PART II   EXPERIMENTS AND APPLICATIONS

Preface and acknowledgements

This monograph combines research on decision making under uncertainty and research on expectations, two fields that have been moving closer together over recent decades. Current perception on expectations and their effects continues to rest to a large extent on the notion of unbounded rationality. This book takes human cognitive limitations seriously and documents many forms and effects of bounded rationality important for both the economic researcher and the economic policy maker. The text offers a solid and easily accessible introduction to the issues by blending theoretical analysis with experimental studies. The book targets researchers as well as economists working in business and government and the text is also suitable for students taking upper-level undergraduate and graduate courses on behavioural economics, the economics of uncertainty and information, forecasting and experimental economics. The text aims to achieve a balance between a textbook and a research monograph. Part I presents the basic tools and theoretical models necessary to understanding rational and boundedly rational expectations and their role in economic life. Every chapter in the first part of the book ends with suggestions for further reading. Part II of the book explores the fascinating insights behavioural economics – the study of actual human decision makers – has to offer. In this part a series of innovative experiments illustrate how bounded rationality affects economic behaviour and performance. The following provides a short survey of the various chapters:

Chapter 1 acquaints the reader with the reasons why forecasting – the formation of expectations – is essential to economic life. Using the Arrow-Debreu model of complete markets we identify production lags as one among several decisive factors. Chapter 2 introduces the concept of expected utility maximization and its applications. Expected utility maximization is shown to be a flexible and powerful tool for the analysis of decision making under uncertainty. Chapter 3 clarifies the effects of heterogeneity in agents' expectations on market outcomes. In particular, it is shown that individuals' forecasting errors even matter when these errors average out in the population. Chapter 4 investigates the conditions under which forecasting should be replaced by other strategies of dealing with uncertainty. When expectations are costly to form, behavioural alternatives like diversification of projects may supersede forecasting. Chapter 5 presents time series models with expectations. Here goods and asset markets are studied under various forms of expectations heuristics and under rational expectations.

Chapter 6 starts the analysis of human behaviour in experimental settings. Here, people's difficulties with expectations formation based on costly information are documented. Chapter 7 shows how the form of bounded rationality documented in Chapter 6 can be incorporated into cost–benefit analysis: we apply the finding of underacquisition of costly information to the public policy question of who should finance satellite-based information. Chapter 8 turns to pattern recognition as an important behavioural tendency in time series extrapolation. The patterns of runs and zigzag movements turn out to be the most important patterns subjects rely on when forming expectations. Chapter 9 describes a more advanced experiment designed to elicit pattern-based expectations in a more general setting. These expectations data are applied to model financial markets where pattern extrapolation drives prices and we assess how well this model fits data of exchange rates and stock prices. Chapter 10 turns to the study of coordination of activities when decisions are decentralized and anticipation-based. Under such circumstances coordination functions poorly and centralized decision making has advantages way above what theorizing based on perfect rationality would suggest. Chapter 11 analyses an important issue in monetary economics. In this final chapter a model of a monetary economy is developed to investigate the role played by expectations in the determination of the general level of prices. The laboratory study shows that the quantity theory of money appears to be an economic relationship that is robust to agents' deviations from perfect rationality.

Five of the chapters appearing in this book are revised and extended versions of articles previously published. Chapter 3 is based on 'Price and output effects of heterogeneous expectations' (published in *Swiss Journal of Economics and Statistics*, **132** (2), 1996, pp. 207–22, Swiss Society of Economics and Statistics). Chapter 4 is based on 'Forecasting among alternative strategies in the management of uncertainty' (published in *Managerial and Decision Economics*, **19** (3), 1998, pp. 179–87, John Wiley & Sons). Chapter 6 is based on 'Acquisition of costly information: an experimental study' (published in *Journal of Economic Behavior and Organization*, **46** (2), 2001, pp. 193–208, Elsevier). Chapter 7 is based on 'Applied welfare economics with bounded rationality: public policies toward remote sensing' (published in *International Advances in Economic Research*, **11** (1), February 2005, pp. 39–47, International Atlantic Economic Society). Chapter 8 is based on 'Pattern recognition and procedurally rational expectations' (published in *Journal of Economic Behavior and Organization*, **37** (1), 1998, pp. 71–90, Elsevier).

I would like to thank the numerous colleagues who have at some point during the research that went into this book helped me to clarify issues and resolve problems. In particular I wish to mention Ernst Baltensperger, Richard Day, Sean Flynn, Marina Groner, Rudolf Groner, Carlos Lenz, Georg Rich, David Grether, Jürg Niehans, David Rumelhart and Sheldon White. Pierre-Andre Gericke and Enrico Schumann provided able research assistance. Ruth Parham has helped to improve the style of the text and Susann Storz has solved many administrative problems. Finally, I want to thank Sylke for her moral support that made writing this book an enjoyable experience.

PART I

Models and tools

1. Markets and expectations

1.1 INTRODUCTION

This chapter addresses a straightforward question. Why do consumers and producers form expectations? To a layperson this question is easy to answer: clearly, we have to make decisions that affect our situation (welfare) in the future. Hence, it seems obvious that we need to form expectations of the likely future in order to take the right actions today. To the professional economist the matter is less clear because, typically, economists are accustomed to work with a theory of markets in which the formation of expectations is not an a priori necessity. This theoretical environment is the world of complete markets with contingent claims (see Arrow, 1953; Debreu, 1959). In this framework all goods ever produced in the future are traded at one point in time, say today, and the future evolves according to contracts written today. Given the uncertainty of the world, agents in this environment have to write contracts (contingent claims) for many different circumstances or contingencies.

Hence, to take an example, what a consumer is prepared to pay in this fictitious world for a vacation to a specific destination at a specific date in the future differs depending on different conditions regarding temperature, humidity and a number of other parameters. In the Arrow–Debreu set-up the consumer bids for (and commits himself to) many different contracts even for just this vacation and he offers different sums of money (or goods) in return depending on the circumstances ruling on the day of his planned departure. Producers of vacations behave similarly and the list of contingencies they want to specify will encompass variables like the costs of labour and capital. Clearly, in this world the vast majority of all contracts will have no consequences simply because the specified contingencies never materialize. The important point, however, is that since all contingencies are covered the described perfect market economy would make it unnecessary to form expectations regarding the likelihood of events. Several reasons stand against the general empirical relevance of this framework: first, the sheer number of contracts that would have to be considered could not be handled by any human mind. Second, the costs of writing and verifying all these contracts would be excessive. These are two key reasons why in reality contracts cannot be written for all

3

circumstances and why expectations influence the content of deals actually made.

Moreover, many contingencies important to consumers and producers are of an individual type: the personal income situation, the existing relationship ties, and even moods will affect an individual's preferences. Since many of these contingencies are under the control of the individual consumer or the individual producer they give rise to adverse selection and moral hazard problems, an issue intensely debated in economic contract theory since Akerlof's (1970) contribution. Yet other contingencies are not objectively measurable and for that reason cannot be part of contracts. For all these circumstances that either cannot be objectively measured or can be influenced by the agent on one side of the contract, offers and demands will depend on expectations regarding these circumstances. The above discussion indicates some of the impediments to the implementation of a perfect market economy. In what follows, we elaborate where expectations enter even where the described limitations to the state preference framework do not apply. Thus, we address the conditions where the formation of expectations or the selection of a decision rule under uncertainty is indispensable.

1.2 A SIMPLE SET-UP

Consider a world lasting for two periods (period one and period two) with two possible states (circumstances) in the second period and two goods produced. The two circumstances are sun and rain. The two goods produced are termed 'sun goods' (that is, umbrellas) and 'rain goods' (that is, sandbags). Preferences of individuals are assumed to be identical and consumers value both goods under both circumstances: in good weather umbrellas are more highly estimated than in bad weather but even when it rains umbrellas are of some use. The same holds for sandbags in sunny weather. Consumption only takes place in period two. Hence, the state-contingent commodities that are traded in period one for delivery in period two are: (1) umbrellas with sun; (2) umbrellas with rain; (3) sandbags with sun; and (4) sandbags with rain. We assume that one umbrella takes the same amount of work (the only resource considered in the model) to produce as one sandbag. Hence, the budget line shown in Figure 1.1 has a slope of minus one.

Tastes of consumers differ depending on the weather: in good weather the indifference curves describing the utility of the representative consumer will have a slope of less than minus one (that is, will be steeper) when evaluated at their intersection with the 45 degree line. In bad weather the indifference

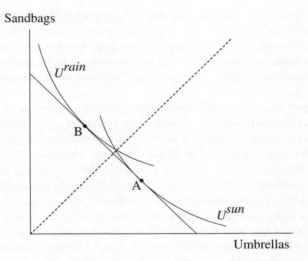

Sandbags

U^{rain}

B

A

U^{sun}

Umbrellas

Figure 1.1   The choice of goods under different contingencies

curves will have a slope of more than minus one (that is, will be flatter) when similarly evaluated. This is shown in Figure 1.1 where the utility for the two contingencies are represented by one indifference curve for each possible state denoted by U^{rain} and U^{sun}, respectively. In fact, the drawn indifference curve for each type of weather marks the highest attainable utility level under any type of weather. This optimum of utility is reached when the (state-contingent) production mix is chosen where the relevant indifference curve is tangential to the budget line. Hence, in the case of sunshine an output mix with more than 50 per cent of umbrellas is optimal and in rain a mix with more than 50 per cent of sandbags is optimal. This is indicated by points A and B.

1.3   THE ROLE OF PRODUCTION LAGS

Consider now what happens in the simplest case where there is sufficient time for the production of goods between the point in time at which the prevailing weather condition is ascertained and the point at which consumption takes place. In this case people wake up in the morning, ascertain the type of weather and produce the optimal mix of goods depending on the prevailing conditions. This is the case without binding production lags. Turn now toward market functioning. The market for state-contingent commodities is a futures market operative in period one. In the case without binding production lags the relative price of the two goods determined in the futures market for delivery in the second period is one. If a spot market existed in period two the spot price would also be one. Clearly, with all agents identical there would be no scope for exchanges in the spot market and thus, under the present circumstances, such a market is unnecessary.

Now, consider the more realistic case where production has to be started before contingencies are ascertained. This is the case with binding production lags. In our model this means that what is consumed in period two has to be produced in period one. Under these circumstances the production decision will by necessity depend on expectations regarding the weather. Take as a starting point the possibility that agents simply make a point prediction. That is, agents believe either weather or sun to prevail. Figure 1.2 shows the case where all agents predict that it will rain in period two and hence produce according to point B. If in fact it rains, this output mix is optimal *ex post*. Moreover, with rain the relative price of the two goods in a possible spot market remains one. Now consider the case where agents expect otherwise. They predict the sun to shine when in fact it rains. This is the case where the weather proves predictions to be wrong. In this case agents have opted for A when production at B would have been optimal. In this case utility is clearly diminished by this misjudgement. Turning again to market outcomes we find that now a spot market (although not affecting anybody's welfare in the present case) would determine a different price than the futures market. On the spot market sandbags fetch a higher price than in the futures market and umbrellas sell at a discount. This higher spot price of sandbags relative to umbrellas can be seen in Figure 1.2 in the slope of the line that is tangential to the indifference curve in point A. With all agents identical this is the equilibrium price because it makes excess demands and excess supplies of the two goods equal to zero. All other relative prices would induce consumers to oversupply either umbrellas or sandbags. Likewise we can analyse the case where all agents predict sunny weather. Figure 1.3 provides the details for this case. Chapter 2 will offer an algebraic treatment of these issues.

1.4   THE MAXIMIN RULE AND EXPECTED UTILITY MAXIMIZATION

As just mentioned, point expectations can have unpleasant effects: if expectations are wrong the outcome in terms of utility can be much lower than in the case of correct anticipations. Let us consider a simple behavioural alternative for decision making under uncertainty. It is the 'maximin

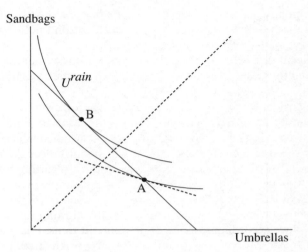

Figure 1.2   Outcomes in the spot market with different expectations in case of rain

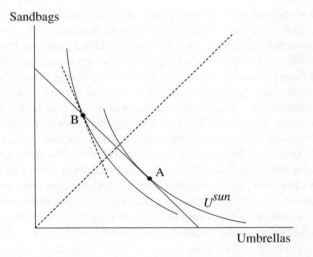

Figure 1.3   Outcomes in the spot market with different expectations in case of sun

principle'. This rule does not yet build on frequencies and probabilities of outcomes. According to the maximin rule the decision maker chooses an output mix that maximizes his utility in the worst possible scenario. In the set-up described this calls for a production mix represented by point C in

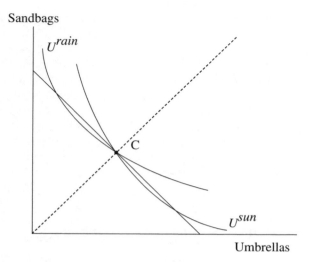

Sandbags

U^{rain}

C

U^{sun}

Umbrellas

Figure 1.4   Choice according to the maximin criterion

Figure 1.4. Any deviation from C on the production frontier in one case (sun or rain) generates lower utility than indicated by the utility curves going through C. If all agents follow the maximin principle then the price in the spot market equals the slope of the relevant indifference curve through C and hence always differs from one, although not by as much as in the case with point predictions discussed before. Incidentally, an outcome similar to that under the maximin rule would be observed if agents were to differ with half of all agents believing with certainty that sun was coming and acting accordingly and the other half sure of coming rain. In this case with heterogeneous expectations the total production of the economy is also equally split into sun goods and rain goods. In contrast to the cases discussed before, in a world with heterogeneous expectations there would be active trading in the spot market. In a situation with rain, for example, agents who had expected and prepared for rain would sell some of their sandbags for more than one-to-one for umbrellas and in the process would increase their own as well as their trading partners' utilities.

The maximin criterion is a reasonable decision rule for situations where little or nothing is known regarding the likelihood of outcomes (see Wald, 1950). However, the maximin principle loses attractiveness if agents face the same situation repeatedly. With repetition people learn about the relative frequencies of rain and sun and can raise their utility by taking these frequencies into account. The principle of expected utility maximization is the straightforward application of this idea. The next chapter will offer a detailed description of the expected utility framework. Here it suffices to state that this decision rule proposes a weighting of utilities in different states of the world with the probabilities of these states. In the context of our model this implies a production mix that maximizes the probability-weighted utility outcomes. For example, with the probabilities of sun and rain generally accepted and equal (that is, each state has probability one-half) the market outcome with expected utility maximizers would coincide with the outcome under the maximin rule. When probabilities are not linked one-to-one to measured frequencies of states (for example, with only few observations available) agents will weigh in their prior beliefs when forming what is then called subjective probabilities. Under such circumstances probability assessments may vary widely across agents.

1.5 SUMMARY AND FURTHER READING

This chapter illustrates the conditions that make the forming of expectations necessary. We start by describing the difficulties a perfect market economy would encounter in practice: the sheer number of possible contingencies or states of the world makes it impossible to organize markets for all state-contingent commodities. Further, contingencies that are not objectively measured give rise to moral hazard problems and hence cannot be written into state-contingent contracts. Hence, these non-contractible elements by necessity become the subject of individual expectations formation. Besides these points it is shown that the fact that production takes time is a key reason why looking into the future is important. Without binding production lags the formation of expectations and plans would be unnecessary and living from day to day would be optimal.

Important concepts used in this chapter are discussed in much more detail in a number of excellent books. Contingent commodities and the issue of resource allocation under uncertainty are made very accessible in Champsaur and Milleron (1983, Part VIII). The analytics of uncertainty and information are treated in great detail in Hirshleifer and Riley (1992) and Eeckhoudt et al. (2005). The topic barely introduced here of subjective probability is the theme of an impressive volume edited by Wright and Ayton (1994). The wider issue of how uncertainty affects market functioning (for example, the question of how markets deal with moral hazard) is featured in books by Salanie (1997) and Bolton and Dewatripont (2005).

2. Expected utility maximization

2.1 INTRODUCTION

This chapter lays the groundwork for the understanding of the expected utility model of decision making. The concept of expected utility maximization goes back to Daniel Bernoulli who first proposed it in 1738 (see Bernoulli, [1738] 1954) as a solution to the famous St Petersburg Paradox of gambling. In the twentieth century expected utility was put on a more rigorous behavioural basis by von Neumann and Morgenstern (1947).[1] In this chapter we start with a classical interpretation of expected utility on the lines of Bernoulli. The classical approach presumes the existence of a cardinal utility function for the individual whose decision under uncertainty is to be modelled. It proceeds by stating that the individual maximizes the probability-weighted utility outcome of his choices. Behaviour so described and its effects can be illustrated within the set-up of the market model introduced in Chapter 1.

2.2 UTILITIES AND PROBABILITIES

Here we study the allocation problem introduced in the previous chapter with binding production lags, that is, production decisions have to be made in period one. There are two possible states of the world in period two (sun or rain) and two goods (umbrellas and sandbags). In the following we take all agents to be identical in their tastes and probability assessments. Hence, there is no need to carry subscripts for individuals through the analysis that follows. We turn to the output determination first. Consider for the sake of simplicity that the form of the agent's utility functions is logarithmic:

$$U^{Sun} = \ln R + \alpha \ln S \qquad (2.1)$$

and

$$U^{Rain} = \alpha \ln R + \ln S \qquad (2.2)$$

Here, R stands for the number of rain goods (for example, sandbags) and S similarly stands for the number of sun goods (for example, umbrellas).

The coefficient α, which is larger than one, shows the extent to which circumstances affect the utility of goods. For the sake of simplicity assume that each person has the capacity to produce one unit of each good if specializing in either of the two goods or any linear combination of these outputs, so that the individual's production possibilities are:

$$S = 1 - R. \tag{2.3}$$

The elements described so far indicate that agents can act independently (everybody acting like Robinson Crusoe) and hence production decisions can be described without introducing markets yet. We assume the probabilities of the two outcomes to be the same (that is, one-half). The representative individual maximizes the sum of probability-weighted utility levels under both possible outcomes:

$$\text{Max}E(U) = \frac{1}{2}[\ln R + \alpha \ln (1 - R)] + \frac{1}{2}[\alpha \ln R + \ln (1 - R)], \tag{2.4}$$

with respect to R. The first-order condition for this problem leads to the optimal level of rain goods produced:

$$R = \frac{\frac{1}{2}(1 + \alpha)}{1 + \alpha} = \frac{1}{2}. \tag{2.5}$$

From (2.3) it is clear that the production of sun goods is similarly one half. Not surprisingly then, the representative agent chooses a fifty-fifty mix of sun and rain goods. Next, we turn to markets and the determination of prices.

2.3 MARKETS AND EQUILIBRIUM

We can use the described set-up to study the determination of market prices even when agents are identical and as a result markets, in principle, are redundant because no transactions will occur.[2] In the futures market of period one the equilibrium relative price between sun goods and rain goods is one because anybody can offer an exchange of sun goods for rain goods at par. However, in the spot market of period two the relative price of the two goods will never be one. Why is this so? Consider, for example, what happens when the weather turns wet. Then agents will maximize the utility function (2.2) relative to the following budget constraint:

$$S = \frac{1}{2} + \pi_r\left(\frac{1}{2} - R\right). \tag{2.6}$$

Here π_r stands for the spot price in rainy times of rain goods expressed in sun goods (that is, the number of sun goods traded for one unit of rain good). The resulting spot demand for rain goods then is:

$$R = \frac{1}{2} \frac{\alpha(1 + \pi_r)}{\pi(1 + \alpha)}. \tag{2.7}$$

Together with the supply of rain goods determined in period one given in (2.5) this condition gives the equilibrium spot price of rain goods expressed in sun goods:

$$\pi_r = \alpha. \tag{2.8}$$

By similar analysis we find that in sunny weather the spot price of rain goods is:

$$\pi_s = 1/\alpha. \tag{2.9}$$

This concludes the analytical treatment of the simple market set-up introduced in Chapter 1 under expected utility maximization. Of course the analysis would become more complicated if agents were not identical. This applies particularly when beliefs (that is, probability assessments) are heterogeneous. With heterogeneous probability assessments agents' expected utility levels become a function of expected benefits from future market transactions. Hence, the subjectively expected spot price affects the agent's production decision and thereby influences the spot price. We will return to the diversity of agents in Chapter 3 where the effects of heterogeneous expectations are assessed in a simple production economy.

2.4   EXPECTED UTILITY ACCORDING TO VON NEUMANN–MORGENSTERN

Many theorists perceive it to be a flaw that the classical version of expected utility is not built on agents' revealed preferences for uncertain outcomes. This limitation can at least in principle be overcome by linking cardinal utility with preferences over lotteries as proposed by von Neumann and Morgenstern (1947). This derivation of the utility function offers a rigorous link between revealed preferences of an individual and his choices as predicted by the theory. We concentrate here on the utility of income and thereby abstract from the problem of allocating income to different possible uses. This means we present a theory of decision making that covers choices over alternatives that generate different income levels in different states. Formally we denote income as a random variable with a density function describing the probability for each income value. For illustration we work with a discrete version where income (Y) is written as the vector:

$$Y = [y_1, y_2, \ldots y_n], \tag{2.10}$$

where the numbers 1 to n denote the possible states of the world and $y_1, y_2, \ldots y_n$ are the income levels in the respective states. The probabilities of the different states (states are indexed by j) are:

$$p_1, p_2, \ldots p_n \text{ with } \sum_{j=1}^{n} p_j = 1. \tag{2.11}$$

Expected income then is:

$$E(Y) \equiv \bar{Y} \equiv \mu_Y = \sum_{j=1}^{n} y_j p_j. \tag{2.12}$$

Imagine as an example an individual who is offered the alternative of operating a store with the following two possible daily income values in dollars:

$$Y = [0, 400], \tag{2.13}$$

with the corresponding probability values of:

$$p(0) = 0.5, p(400) = 0.5. \tag{2.14}$$

Expected income for this alternative is:

$$E(Y) = 0.5 \cdot 0 + 0.5 \cdot 400 = 200. \tag{2.15}$$

The simplest rule for choosing among alternatives would be to take the choice that maximizes expected income. In accordance with this a decision maker who is offered the above-described income opportunity alongside the alternative to earn an income of \$199 with certainty would choose the uncertain alternative. That is, she would run the store and would bear the uncertainty of income of this pursuit for just a marginal advantage in income. This behaviour is termed risk neutral. Many studies indicate that this is not how the majority of individuals and households behave. However, for the description of firm behaviour the model of expected income maximization is frequently used in both theoretical and empirical studies.[3]

The more general proposition compared to expected income maximization is that decision makers maximize their expected von Neumann–Morgenstern utility. The von Neumann–Morgenstern utility function is not simply stated

but is derived from revealed preferences of agents over different income lotteries. Formally, the choice criterion is:

$$MaxE[U_i(Y)] = \sum_{j=1}^{n} p_j U_i(y_j). \qquad (2.16)$$

The cardinal von Neumann–Morgenstern utility function $U_i(y)$ of an individual can be derived by proposing different income lotteries to the individual whose choices are to be modelled. As it turns out the utilities thus
derived are probability values. For our example the method for eliciting
these utilities proceeds by presenting various lotteries where the two possible pay-offs are always zero and 400. For any income level (y) in the range
between zero and 400 the individual is asked the following question: what
probability (f) would have to be associated with the state generating 400 in
the lottery so that you would just be indifferent between the proposed
lottery and that income level for certain? Expressed formally this is:

$$[1 - f(y)] \cdot 0 + f(y) \cdot 400 \sim y, \qquad (2.17)$$

where $\sim$ indicates indifference. The $f(y)$ value thus elicited is the von
Neumann–Morgenstern utility of the income value y. Suppose, for
example, that the questioning of an individual would result in a utility function as displayed in Figure 2.1.[4]
    The question now is, how can it be that we can consistently assess the pref-
erences of this individual over various lotteries each with many different
pay-offs between zero and 400 given that in the questioning described above

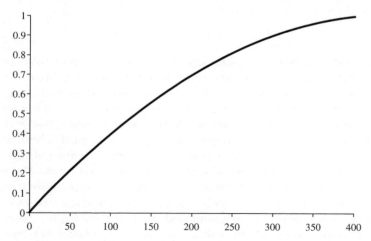

Figure 2.1   An individual's von Neumann–Morgenstern utility function

Table 2.1   Lotteries and compound lotteries

Lottery A: Pay-off	Valued equally as lottery	Lottery has a probability of
50	[0,0.7875;400,0.2125]	0.4
150	[0,0.4375;400,0.5625]	0.5
300	[0,0.1000;400,0.9000]	0.1
Lottery B: Pay-off	Valued equally as lottery	Lottery has a probability of
100	[0,0.6000;400,0.4000]	0.8
200	[0,0.3000;400,0.7000]	0.2

only preferences between a lottery with just two possible pay-offs are elicited? How can it be that the von Neumann–Morgenstern utility function should consistently predict the individual's choices over several and possibly complicated alternatives? To answer these questions we look at an example with the following two lotteries offered for comparison: lottery A pays 50 with a probability of 0.4, 150 with a probability of 0.5, and 300 with a probability of 0.1 written as $L^A = [50,0.4;150,0.5;300,0.1]$. Compare this to lottery B written as $L^B = [100,0.8;200,0.2]$. The two alternatives are made comparable by compounding them to simpler lotteries that are directly comparable. This is done by recurring to the preferences of the individual. For each possible income level (for example, 50 in lottery A) we know which lottery with pay-offs of zero or 400 leaves the individual indifferent. Accordingly, each income value in a lottery (for example, 50) can be represented by a lottery with outcomes zero and 400. Consider lotteries A and B in turn, as shown in Table 2.1.

The lotteries in the middle column are then compounded into single final lotteries (one for lottery A and B, respectively) with pay-offs of zero and 400 by multiplying the probabilities (that is, the von Neumann–Morgenstern utilities selected by the individual) with the respective probability of the pay-off and adding the resulting numbers to find the overall probabilities of the outcomes zero and 400. For the two lotteries A and B the thus compounded lotteries are $L_c^A = [0,0.54375;400,0.45625]$ and $L_c^B = [0,0.5400;400,0.4600]$. The subscript c stands for compounded lottery. In the logic of the von Neumann–Morgenstern calculus an individual will then choose the alternative that has the higher probability of the high pay-off (here 400). In this case this is lottery B. Note that the expected value of income for lottery B (120) is lower than that from lottery A (125). Hence, the individual whose von Neumann–Morgenstern utility function is displayed in Figure 2.1 would – given her risk aversion – prefer alternative B which is the choice with the lower expected pay-off of the two possibilities. To this individual the higher expected income of alternative A does not compensate for the risk of A.

This example also permits a clarification of the concept of the 'certainty equivalent' of a lottery (that is, of an uncertain income alternative). The certainty equivalent of a lottery is that level of income that has to be offered to the individual with certainty in order to generate the same utility as the lottery. Formally, the certainty equivalent CE of a lottery L is that level of income that satisfies the condition:

$$f(CE) = E[f(L)]. \tag{2.18}$$

The certainty equivalents of the two lotteries A and B thus calculated are $CE^A = 116.46$ and $CE^B = 117.59$, respectively. To show that $CE^B > CE^A$ is yet another way to indicate that the individual considered here would prefer alternative B over alternative A. Moreover, these certainty equivalents can be used to evaluate how much this individual would (at the maximum) be willing to forego in expected income for either of the two lotteries if she could exchange it to a fixed income payment: at the utmost our individual would be willing to pay a risk premium of 8.54 (that is, $125 - 116.46$) to someone who would offer her a certain income in exchange for lottery A. For lottery B in turn she would offer a risk premium of 2.41 (that is, $120 - 117.59$).

With a linear von Neumann–Morgenstern utility function an individual is indifferent to risk (that is, is risk neutral). In this case the ordering of expected von Neumann–Morgenstern utilities for different alternatives is always the same as the ordering of expected income levels. It is only in this case that the spread of pay-offs does not affect the individual's choice and her utility level. If the utility function shows diminishing marginal utility of income as shown in Figure 2.1 (the case of risk aversion) expected utility declines as pay-offs deviate more from their mean value. Clearly, with a utility function displaying increasing marginal von Neumann–Morgenstern utility (the case of risk loving) expected utility rises with increasing risk. The next section clarifies the trade-off between mean income and risk by focusing on the case of risk aversion.

2.5   VARIANCE OF INCOME AS MEASURE OF RISK

Consider the simple case of a lottery offering the two pay-offs of 100 and 300 with probabilities of one-half each. In this case expected utility can be graphically determined as shown in Figure 2.2. It is the average of the two

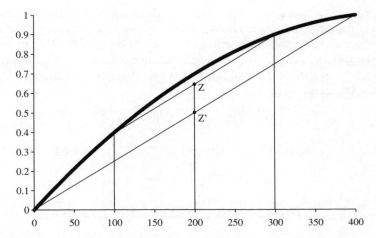

Figure 2.2   Diminishing expected utility with rising risk

utility levels at incomes 100 and 300 as displayed by the level of utility (0.65, that is, midway between 0.4 and 0.9) at point Z. Consider what happens when the two possible pay-offs are zero and 400 instead of 100 and 300. In this case expected income remains unchanged (at 200) but the standard deviation of income doubles. As a result expected utility would drop as indicated by the lower level of utility attained at point Z' compared to point Z in Figure 2.2.

We can be more specific concerning the effect of the income risk by noting that for any random number (here represented by the symbol for income) for which the mean and the variance are well defined the following relationship holds:

$$E(Y^2) = \bar{Y}^2 + Var(Y). \tag{2.19}$$

This expression for the mathematical expectation of the square of a random variable is very helpful when assessing expected utility in this case which turns out to be:[5]

$$E[U(Y)] = E[aY - bY^2] = a\bar{Y} - bE(Y^2) = a\bar{Y} - b\bar{Y}^2 - b\sigma_Y^2. \tag{2.20}$$

Hence, we see that in this case expected utility is a quadratic function of expected income and a negatively linear function of the variance of income. Here, then, we have a case where maximization of expected utility can be captured by a mean-variance representation. However, it has to be noted that the variance is a sufficient statistic for income risk in only two cases: the first case is the quadratic utility function described above and the second case is the situation where (allowing for any form of the utility function) income values are normally distributed (see Tobin, 1958). We can verify numerically the precision of the mean-variance representation of expected utility by considering our two lotteries A and B again. According to (2.20) for the two cases we have:

$$E[U(L^A)] = a\bar{Y}^A - b(\bar{Y}^A)^2 - b\sigma^2_{Y^A}$$

$$= 0.0045 \cdot 125 - 0.000005 \cdot (125^2 + 5625) = 0.45625 \qquad (2.21)$$

$$E[U(L^B)] = a\bar{Y}^B - b(\bar{Y}^B)^2 - b\sigma^2_{Y^B}$$

$$= 0.0045 \cdot 120 - 0.000005 \cdot (120^2 + 1600) = 0.4600 \qquad (2.22)$$

Comparing these numbers with the utilities of the compounded lotteries derived before we notice an exact match: the level of utility for income of 400 is one for each lottery and this level is attained with compounded probabilities of 0.45625 in the case of lottery A and with 0.46 in the case of lottery B.

2.6   MEASURES OF RISK AVERSION

It is evident from Figure 2.2 that the evaluation of an uncertain income stream is determined: (1) by the spread of payments (that is, by risk); and (2) by the curvature of the individual's von Neumann–Morgenstern utility function (that is, by risk aversion). It is the curvature of the utility function that shows the risk aversion of the individual. Several measures of risk aversion are regularly used in the literature: The measure of absolute risk aversion is:

$$MARA = \delta = -\frac{U''(Y)}{U'(Y)}. \qquad (2.23)$$

The measure of relative risk aversion is:

$$MRRA = \theta = -Y\frac{U''(Y)}{U'(Y)}. \qquad (2.24)$$

For the example of the quadratic utility function we have $\delta = 2b/(a - 2bY)$ and $\theta = 2b/[(a/Y) - 2b]$. For both measures of risk aversion the case of risk indifference or risk neutrality (that is, the case of a linear von Neumann–Morgenstern utility function) is marked with risk-aversion measures of zero. The next section shows an interesting case where the measure of absolute risk aversion fully captures the agent's preferences toward risk.

2.7 PORTFOLIO SELECTION AS EXEMPLARY APPLICATION OF EXPECTED UTILITY MAXIMIZATION

The demand for assets of different risk characteristics is one of the classic applications of expected utility maximization (see Markowitz, 1952, 1959; Tobin, 1958). Let us look at an individual who has the opportunity to allocate his wealth to two possible assets. One asset is a risk-free asset called 'bond' and the other is a risky asset called 'stock'. The bond yields a safe gross return denoted by I whereas the return on the stock is risky and yields a mean gross return of $\bar{R}$ with a variance of σ_R^2. The portfolio allocation problem is simplified by assuming that the individual under consideration consumes all wealth one period into the future. Thus, we have a two-period problem where the investor maximizes his expected utility. The second-period total pay-off is denoted by Y. Assuming a quadratic von Neumann–Morgenstern utility function the individual maximizes:

$$E[U(Y)] = E[aY - bY^2] \qquad (2.25)$$

subject to:

$$Y = xWR + (1 - x)WI, \qquad (2.26)$$

with respect to x. Here x is the fraction of stocks in the portfolio and $1 - x$ is the fraction of bonds. W is the initial level of wealth. The variance of the second-period pay-off is:

$$\sigma_Y^2 = x^2 W^2 \sigma_R^2. \qquad (2.27)$$

Solving the optimality condition for x and multiplying x with the individual's level of initial wealth leads to the following demand function for stocks:

$$xW = -\frac{a - 2b\bar{Y}}{2b\sigma_R^2}(\bar{R} - I) = \frac{1}{\bar{\delta}\sigma_R^2}(\bar{R} - I), \qquad (2.28)$$

where $\bar{\delta}$ is the measure of risk aversion evaluated at the mean level of Y. Here we can see clearly how risk (that is, the variance of the stock return) interacts with risk aversion to determine the demand for a risky asset: the lower risk and risk aversion, on the one hand, and the higher the difference in expected returns in favour of the risky asset, on the other hand, the higher is the individual's demand for stocks.

2.8   SUMMARY AND FURTHER READING

Expected utility maximization is a powerful tool for the analysis of decision making under uncertainty. With this approach we can study how agents' assessments of utilities and probabilities interact to determine market outcomes. The expected utility framework also helps to clarify why we find expected pay-off variables in behavioural functions (like, for example, the expected return in the demand for stocks) even when agents are risk averse. According to the expected utility framework the level of risk and of risk aversion is seen as affecting the parameters of such behavioural functions.

Expected utility, its applications and alternatives are the subject of an extensive literature. Hirshleifer and Riley (1992) offer a good introduction and a short survey of the empirically documented deviations of behaviour from expected utility maximization. Schoemaker (1982) and Machina (1989) provide additional interesting material concerning variants, applications, limitations and extensions of the expected utility model. Prospect theory proposed by Kahneman and Tversky (1979) and Tversky and Kahneman (1992) and the approach suggested by Gilboa and Schmeidler (1995) present alternatives to the expected utility model which have received much attention in the literature.

NOTES

1. See Hamouda and Rowley (1996, Chapter 2) for more historical background.
2. With everybody the same there will be no trades on these markets. Despite this no-trade feature such models (see also Lucas, 1978) are useful tools for discussing price determination.
3. See, for example, Cothren (1983) and Lundberg and Startz (1983).
4. Incidentally, the curve displayed is quadratic. That is, the function $f(y) = ay - by^2$ is used. The concrete parameterization displayed is $f(y) = 0.0045y - 0.000005y^2$.
5. Here it is helpful to note some rules for the calculus of expectations: If c is a constant $Ec = c$ and $E(cY) = cE(Y)$. Further, we also note that for variances the following holds: $Var(cY) = c^2 Var(Y)$.

3. Effects of heterogeneous expectations

3.1 INTRODUCTION

This chapter explores the effects of heterogeneity of expectations. While heterogeneity of expectations is widely acknowledged (see, for example, Katona, 1946; Ito, 1990; Levine, 1993; Dominitz, 1998; Ciccone, 2005) it is less clear whether heterogeneity matters for economic analysis. One common proposition is that individual errors in expectations do not matter for economic outcomes as long as the expectations of the population are on average unbiased. As David Begg (1982, p. 63) puts it, 'one can appeal to the law of large numbers which argues that individual idiosyncrasies are likely to cancel out in the aggregate, leaving average behavior rather closer to the implications of the (rational expectations) theory'.[1] This suggests that we should rely on the predictions of models built on the assumption that all individuals can be represented by a single rational individual. This notion has been widely debated in the literature and many of its limitations are already recognized.[2] Evidence on population expectations that, in their mean, are biased have been documented in the empirical literature in various forms. See, for example, the literature on the rational expectations hypothesis (such as, Figlewski and Wachtel, 1981; Lovell, 1986). Keynes's (1936) notion of waves of optimistic and pessimistic sentiment captures the idea that aggregate bias can change its direction over time. Evidence gathered by psychologists and economists indicates that people tend to overestimate their own abilities (see Frieze et al., 1978; Pruitt and Gitman, 1987; Tyebjee, 1987; Heine and Lehman, 1995; Eysenck and Derakshan, 1997; Arnett, 2000). Thus, while expectations may be biased towards pessimism some of the time, on average they seem to be biased towards optimism.[3]

We analyse a model of land use and investigate how heterogeneous expectations influence land rent and production.[4] The basic set-up follows Niehans (1997). In our model individuals produce a commodity by means of a factor of production called 'land'. A market operates on which landowners can lend their land to other producers. Land stands exemplary for factors of production whose input levels can be varied by the producer. Dispersion of expectations is captured by modelling two types of individuals: optimists who overpredict and pessimists who underpredict their success.[5] This set-up makes it easy to study the influence of heterogeneity of expectations with a possible disparity of optimists and pessimists in the population. Hence, the model developed here allows for average (or aggregate) bias in either direction. It turns out that the effects of expectations bias critically depend on the definition of this bias. In the present framework two meanings of the term 'aggregate bias' are considered, namely: (1) that there are unequal proportions of optimists and pessimists in the population; and (2) that the sum of expectations errors aggregated over all agents differs from zero.

3.2   THE MODEL

The most concise way of formulating dispersion in expectations (or beliefs) is to assume that there are just two types of individuals, optimists and pessimists, indexed by o and p. The individuals produce a commodity with the variable factor of production land (L). Everybody produces with the same production function:

$$Q_p^{ef} = L_p - \beta L_p^2$$
$$Q_o^{ef} = L_o - \beta L_o^2$$
$$\text{with } 1/(2L^*) > \beta > 0.[6] \tag{3.1}$$

Production is subject to diminishing returns because there is a second factor of production called management skill of which every producer has a fixed amount. The superscript *ef* indicates that this is the effective output produced by an individual. Given that the production functions are the same for all, a socially efficient land use demands that all use the same amount of land. This is called the rational expectations equilibrium since agents with unbiased (that is, correct) expectations would choose this allocation. This is the benchmark against which all emerging allocations will be judged. A land market allows agents to rent land from others who will be, in the present set-up, those with different expectations. The model presented here will show land rent and output as a function of the size of individual errors and the overall composition of the population.

Conceptually, the difference between optimists and pessimists can be captured in various ways. The terms 'optimism' and 'pessimism' are closely tied to the concept of subjective probabilities. This does not mean that a model with optimists and pessimists necessarily has to be a stochastic model. As a matter of fact, the model presented in the main text here is not probabilistic. Appendix 3.1 shows the equivalence of the approach used here with a formulation where probability assessments are the object of disagreement and misjudgement. We avoid the use of probabilities here by assuming that agents have subjective beliefs about a future outcome which is deterministic. In this framework the future is fully predetermined but agents are liable to make errors assessing the quantitative link between the present and the future. Consider as an example the swinging of a hammer, as a test of strength game at a county fair. Here, it is simple to classify individuals into optimists and pessimists. Optimists are those who overpredict their abilities while pessimists underpredict their abilities. Similarly, producers in our model are classified according to their propensity to over- or underpredict their success. Optimists and pessimists both misperceive their productivity: optimists overpredict output at every level of input while pessimists underpredict output. We start by describing the situation of the individuals and the optimization problem. One way to formalize individual expectational errors is the following:[7]

$$Q_p^s = (1 - \alpha)L_p - \beta L_p^2$$
$$Q_o^s = (1 + \alpha)L_o - \beta L_o^2. \tag{3.2}$$

The superscript s denotes that these are subjectively perceived production possibilities.[8] Here, α is a constant equal to or larger than zero ($\alpha = 0$ means rational foresight) that measures the individual error in expectations about productivity. Hence, the assessment of the level of the intercept of the marginal productivity curve is the object of disagreement in this model set-up. The larger α, the more optimists err on the upper side and the more pessimists err on the lower side. The two (subjective) income functions for the two types of individuals are:

$$Y_p^s = Q_p^s - r(L_p - \overline{L})$$
$$Y_o^s = Q_o^s - r(L_o - \overline{L}). \tag{3.3}$$

Here, $\overline{L}$ denotes the land endowment per individual (assumed the same for all) and r is the rental price for land. It is assumed that individuals aim at maximizing their income. After deriving first-order conditions we can write the two land demand functions:

$$L_p = \frac{1 - r - \alpha}{2\beta}$$

$$L_o = \frac{1 - r + \alpha}{2\beta} \tag{3.4}$$

Clearly, optimists (at any interest rate) want to cultivate more land than pessimists. From these demand functions we take the step to the equilibrium on the land market:

$$\theta L_p + (1 - \theta)L_o = \overline{L}, \tag{3.5}$$

where θ denotes the fraction of pessimists and $(1-\theta)$ the fraction of optimists.[9] The resulting equilibrium land rent is:

$$r = 1 - 2\beta\overline{L} + \alpha(1 - 2\theta). \tag{3.6}$$

The first two terms on the right-hand side of (3.6) indicate the rational expectations land rent: the outcome when everybody has correct judgement (that is, $\alpha = 0$). Land rental is lower the higher the fraction of pessimists in the population. The intuition for this is straightforward: pessimists expect low productivity and hence are unwilling to pay much for rented land. The effect of the size of the forecast error depends on whether optimists or pessimists are in the majority. In the former (latter) case a higher α increases (diminishes) land rent. Figure 3.1 gives a three-dimensional display of these results. The simulations underlying the figure are based on the values $\beta = 0.25$ and $\overline{L} = 1$. These numbers lead to a benchmark land rent of 0.5. The maximum of individual errors considered for the figure $\alpha = 0.15$ means an (absolute) error of 20 per cent at the input level $\overline{L} = 1$ and implies land inputs by the two types of agents of $L_p = 0.8$ and $L_o = 1.2$. The same as the rational expectations level of land rent also results when producers make errors (that is, with $\alpha > 0$) but the two types of agents come in equal numbers (that is, $\theta = 0.5$). Thus, the present set-up supports the proposition regarding market equilibrium cited in the introduction to this chapter: any level of heterogeneity of beliefs produces the same outcome as under rational expectations so long as there are equal numbers of optimists and pessimists in the population. Hence, if aggregate bias is measured by the disparity of optimists and pessimists then heterogeneity of expectations does not affect land rent so long as there is no aggregate bias. If, however, absence of aggregate bias means that individual errors cancel out over the whole population, this result does not hold. This becomes apparent when considering that in a situation with $\theta = 0.5$ (the condition for effects of heterogeneity to be neutral with respect to rent) the sum of expectations errors is positive: since optimists use more land than pessimists the typical optimist will overestimate his output by more than the typical pessimist will underestimate his output. The fraction of pessimists necessary for making the sum of expectations errors (at any level of α) equal to zero is the solution of a quadratic equation.[10] The dashed curve on the surface displayed in Figure 3.1 marks the situations with zero aggregate expectations errors and indicates that they are characterized by land rent lower (and declining with rising α) than under rational expectations.

Average output, unlike land rent, is always affected by dispersion of beliefs. Output is the weighted average of optimists' and pessimists' production. In

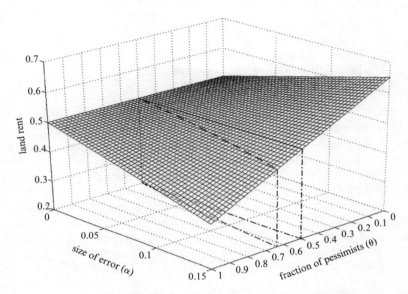

Figure 3.1   Land rent as a function of the size of the individual
expectations error (α) and the fraction of pessimists in
the population (θ)

order to derive it (3.6) is inserted into (3.4) to find the land uses of the two types of individuals and these, in turn, are inserted into (3.1). Per capita output then is:

$$Q = \theta Q_p^{ef} + (1 - \theta) Q_0^{ef}, \tag{3.7}$$

which can be written as

$$Q = \overline{L} - \beta \overline{L}^2 - \frac{\alpha^2}{\beta}(1 - \theta)\theta. \tag{3.8}$$

The first two terms on the right-hand side of equation (3.8) indicate benchmark output while the third term shows the output loss due to expectational error. Output is clearly highest when there are no expectations errors (that is, $\alpha = 0$). However, when there are expectations errors it would be socially desirable to have complete uniformity in opinions (that is, $\theta = 0$ or $\theta = 1$). It does not matter whether all individuals are optimists or pessimists but it is clearly efficient for all individuals to be equal. In this case the market allocates the same amount of land to every individual just as in a situation where all have perfect judgement. The worst case is when, with expectations errors, the two groups of optimists and pessimists are of equal

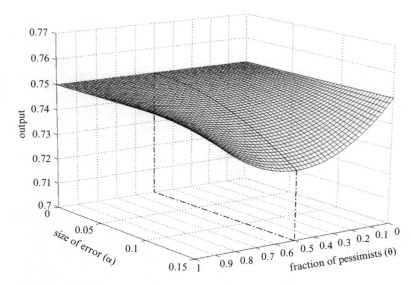

Figure 3.2   Output as a function of the size of the individual expectations error (α) and the fraction of pessimists in the population (θ)

size (that is, $\theta = 0.5$). Figure 3.2 shows output as a function of the two parameters α and θ.[11] If we consider the possibility that, at levels of $\alpha > 0$, the composition of optimists and pessimists is not fifty-fifty, then output increases when the population is biased either toward optimism or toward pessimism. This example shows that it would be wrong to believe that pessimism is necessarily welfare reducing.

3.3   SUMMARY AND FURTHER READING

The most important insight here is that heterogeneity of expectations matters. Output clearly falls with rising expectations errors. This occurs even – and strongly – when there are equal numbers of over- and underpredictors in the economy. This should help overcome the popular notion that market outcomes equal the predictions from rational expectations models so long as individual idiosyncrasies cancel out in the aggregate. Moreover, the analysis indicates that a general assertion of the kind that an economy with a majority of pessimists (that is, underpredictors) is worse off than an economy with a majority of optimists (that is, overpredictors), or the reverse, is untenable. Land rent, unlike output, can remain unaffected by heterogeneous expectations given parity between over- and underpredictors.[12] In summary, both the prices of productive assets of an economy and the output level achieved depend on the ability of producers to make accurate quantitative assessments. Improving this ability through schooling is likely to produce welfare gains. As the analysis of this chapter suggests, similarity of assessments can mitigate the losses due to wrong assessments. Hence, conformity can be a social virtue and individualism can be a burden.

Further sources on the effects of expectations heterogeneity can be found in several sub-areas of economics. Agricultural economics (the starting point in this chapter) has seen various analyses of the effects of heterogeneity: Pope (1981) investigates the effects of dispersion of expectations regarding the prices of agricultural commodities while Brown and Brown (1984) analyse the effects of heterogeneous expectations regarding future land prices on current land prices. Financial economists (for example, De Long et al., 1990) and international economists (for example, Frankel and Froot, 1990) have studied effects of heterogeneity of expectations by modelling the diversity of forecast rules with some agents who forecast rationally while others (called 'noise traders' or 'chartists') follow simple heuristics that lead to systematic forecast errors. Likewise in macroeconomics: Bomfim (2001) reviews and sharpens the analysis of the effects of heterogeneous expectations on aggregate dynamics.

NOTES

1. Text in parenthesis added.
2. Kirman (1992) gives easy access to this literature while Radner's (1982) survey covers many technical points.
3. Waldman (1994) suggests that this may be an optimal response of evolution to maladaptive preferences.
4. The effects on land rent and land price are qualitatively the same if (as a sufficient condition) the interest rate is unaffected by the heterogeneity of beliefs.
5. Niehans's (1997) model of a land market captures differences in beliefs by modelling three types of individuals: optimists, pessimists and realists. He assumes that the fact that an agent's judgement about the future is deficient (that is, he either is an optimist or a pessimist) implies that he obtains less output from a given input than a realist. These assumptions imply that in the Niehans analysis effects of heterogeneity are quite different from the present analysis. In particular, here there is no a priori welfare cost of optimism.
6. L^* is larger than any equilibrium input level considered in the following.
7. Other formulations are possible and the effects of heterogeneity depend on what exactly is the object of misjudgement (see Rötheli, 1996).
8. As a reminder (3.1) describes effective production possibilities.
9. Equation (3.5) follows from

$$n_p L_p + n_o L_o = \overline{L}_{total}$$

where n_p and n_o denote the numbers of pessimists and optimists. The θ in (3.5) then is $n_p/(n_p + n_o)$ and $\overline{L}$ is $\overline{L}_{total}/(n_p + n_o)$, that is, average land supply.

10. The condition that needs to hold for the sum of errors to be zero is

$$\theta = \frac{\alpha - \beta + \sqrt{\alpha^2 + \beta^2}}{2\alpha}.$$

11. The benchmark level of output is 0.75 given the numerical values of $\beta = 0.25$ and $\overline{L} = 1$.
12. If the object of individual errors is something else than the intercept of the marginal product curve this neutrality need not hold (see Rötheli, 1996).

APPENDIX 3.1 MODELLING HETEROGENEITY OF EXPECTATIONS WITH PROBABILITIES

This appendix shows the basic equivalence of the set-up used in this chapter and the state space approach with subjective probabilities. This formulation follows Hey (1984). The individuals in this model variant assign different subjective probabilities to two possible states of the world and maximize expected income (that is, are risk neutral). In what follows individuals and states of the world are described in detail. There are two states of the world: a good state and a bad state. In the bad state the output is just:

$$Q = (1 - g)L - bL^2, \tag{A3.1}$$

while in the good state it is:

$$Q = (1 + g)L - bL^2, \tag{A3.2}$$

where g is a constant larger than zero. Objectively, the two outcomes have the same probability of one-half. However, the two types of individuals assign different subjective probabilities to the two possible states. The pessimist assigns the probability $\gamma > 0.5$ to the bad outcome and the probability $1 - \gamma < 0.5$ to the good outcome. The optimist does just the opposite. The subjectively expected output for the two types of individuals can now be written as:

$$Q_p = [1 - (2\gamma - 1)g]L_p - bL_p^2$$
$$Q_o = [1 + (2\gamma - 1)g]L_o - bL_o^2, \tag{A3.3}$$

where L_p and L_o are the land inputs of the two types of agents. These two equations show the equivalence indicated above: the term $(2\gamma - 1)g$ in (A3.3) plays the same role as α in (3.2). In fact, with $\gamma = 1$, that is, individuals believe fully in the occurrence of one outcome, (A3.3) becomes

$$Q_p = (1 - g)L_p - bL_p^2$$
$$Q_o = (1 + g)L_o - bL_o^2. \tag{A3.4}$$

Hence, g in (A3.4) plays the same role as α in (3.2) and the analysis of the two models becomes interchangeable.

4. Forecasting among alternative strategies under uncertainty

4.1 INTRODUCTION

Chapters 1 and 2 of this book have documented the importance of forming accurate expectations or forecasts. It is time now for an analysis of the optimal behaviour toward an uncertain future when several strategies are available including the option to have no informed forecast. In a basic manner this has already been treated in Chapter 1 with the example of the maximin criterion. The present chapter explores this issue in more detail and shows why the formation of an informed forecast may not be part of an agent's optimal management of uncertainty. In particular we will focus on the alternatives available to an agent who does not bother to predict future outcomes. Relevant pieces that contribute to this analysis were developed by Cooper and Simon (1955) who discussed servo-mechanisms in business applications that substitute for forecasting and by Bowman (1958) who suggested diversification as an alternative to forecasting. A specification of the conditions under which forecasting is dominated by other strategies has been much helped by the contributions of McDonald and Siegel (1986) and Dixit and Pindyck (1994). A cornerstone of their analysis is the concept of the 'option value of waiting'. Waiting with the option to commit to some action (like an investment) later is of value if the expected net present value (ENPV) of an investment to be started sometime in the future (with an enlarged information set) is higher than the ENPV of an investment started in the present. With further strategic choices available this concept is generalized to a ranking of all available behavioural alternatives. Only the strategy that generates the highest ENPV under a given set of circumstances is of value and choosing one of the other alternatives incurs opportunity costs.

In the spirit of this analysis we compare forecasting with the alternative of waiting, that is, letting time reveal information freely that, *ex ante*, would be available only at considerable cost. Besides forecasting and waiting we also consider diversification, switching between projects, eliminating of inferior projects over time, as well as the possibility of going ahead with a project as soon as the ENPV based on common knowledge is positive.

4.2 CHOICE OF STRATEGY

The investment problem analysed here is one frequently encountered in reality: a firm can set up production sites in different locations, possibly in different countries. Alternatively, a firm faces the problem of deciding which of several technologies should be applied for the production of a good. A further variant of the problem occurs when a firm wants to develop a new product: R&D can be pursued along one line or along several lines. In all these cases factors outside the firm's control play a prominent role in determining which location, technology or approach turns out the most successful. The question pursued here is whether under such circumstances the firm should invest resources to make an informed forecast or whether the firm should adopt an alternative strategy. In order to analyse optimal behaviour a stylized version of the decision problem is presented next.

Let us assume that the number of possible projects is limited to two and that these projects are assumed to run over a maximum of two periods. Both projects can be started in period one or in period two. The projects will be terminated after period two because, presumably, new and superior alternatives will become available by then. At that point the decision problem is posed afresh. The decision as to which, if any, project should be operated has to be made at the beginning of each period. At the beginning of period one the two projects look equally promising. However, as period one passes the high productivity project yields a gross return of $\alpha + \phi$ per period while the low productivity project yields a gross return of $\alpha - \phi$. These are the returns that the two projects will generate in the second period as well. Here, α is the expected return and ϕ is the spread parameter (incidentally the standard deviation) measuring the uncertainty of returns. The possible levels of return are common knowledge. Which of the projects is the winner is revealed at the end of period one even if the decision maker chooses not to invest in the first period. The passage of time alone reveals this information.

The decision maker further knows about the alternative strategies he can choose from. The first feasible alternative in the described situation is to totally refrain from investing. The next possibility is to go ahead with either of the two projects and to stick to this choice for the second period. Furthermore, the firm has the alternative to wait until the second period and then to invest in the winning project. Alternatively, the firm can pick one of the projects arbitrarily and switch, if necessary, to the winning project for period two. In this case (occurring with probability one-half) the firm incurs a relocation or switching cost of P^S. Another possible strategy is eliminating. In this case the firm starts both projects in the first period and closes down the less successful operation in the second period. Forecasting is the next alternative to be discussed. We choose the simplest modelling strategy and assume that a fully informative forecast is available at cost P^F.[1] Hence, the firm can buy information that makes it clear from the outset which of the two projects is going to be the winner. In the example of the location decision the forecast cost would amount to the expense of having specialized investigators visit and analyse the competing sites. The last possibility introduced is diversification. Under this strategy the investor starts both projects in period one and sticks to them for two periods.[2]

We assume that a risk-neutral firm faces the same type of choice time and time again over its lifetime. Hence, maximization of the ENPV is the appropriate decision criterion. For the calculation of the ENPVs under the various strategies the returns in period two have to be discounted at the rate ρ. In the following the choice of optimal strategy is studied under two different assumptions concerning cost: (1) fixed set-up costs; and (2) positive operating costs (with zero set-up costs). In the first case running either project involves an installation cost of C per period independent of whether the project is operated for one or two periods; in the latter case in every period a project is operated, costs of the amount V per period have to be borne.

4.2.1 Fixed Set-up Costs

In this subsection we analyse the investment decision when there is a fixed cost for setting up production in either site. In this case the seven available investment strategies yield the following values of expected net present value (Π):

1.   Refraining: $\Pi = 0$

2.   Going ahead: $\Pi = \alpha + \frac{\alpha}{\rho} - C$

3.   Waiting: $\Pi = \frac{\alpha + \phi}{\rho} - C$

4.   Switching: $\Pi = \alpha + \frac{\alpha + \phi}{\rho} - C - \frac{1}{2}P^S$

5.   Eliminating: $\Pi = 2\alpha + \frac{\alpha + \phi}{\rho} - 2C$

6.   Forecasting: $\Pi = \alpha + \phi + \frac{\alpha + \phi}{\rho} - C - P^F$

7.   Diversifying: $\Pi = 2\left(\alpha + \frac{\alpha}{\rho} - C\right)$

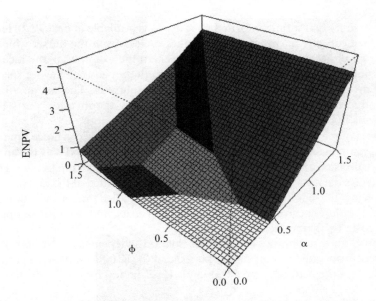

Figure 4.1 ENPV resulting from different strategies with set-up costs

The first point to note is that the strategy of going ahead with one project, if profitable, is always dominated by the strategy of diversification. The obvious reason is that the latter strategy yields twice the ENPV of the former strategy. In order to compare the strategies we choose a graphical display indicating how the choice of optimal investment strategy depends on α and ϕ. Consider the three-dimensional presentation of Figure 4.1. Here, the maximum attainable ENPV level is shown over a range of the parameters α and ϕ. The different shades of the surface indicate ranges of the parameter space where a specific strategy from the list above generates the highest net pay-off. For example, the black region indicates where the strategy of eliminating is optimal. The two-dimensional representation of this display discussed below provides more details. The benchmark case shown in the figure builds on a set of values for C, P^S, P^F and ρ. Specifically, these values are $C = 0.9$, $P^S = 0.5$, $P^F = 1.3$ and $\rho = 1$.[3]

For further clarifications we focus on a two-dimensional display in Figure 4.2. The panel in the middle of Figure 4.2 represents the benchmark case that also underlies Figure 4.1. The surrounding panels show several variations where the level of one of the parameters C, P^S, P^F and ρ is raised and the

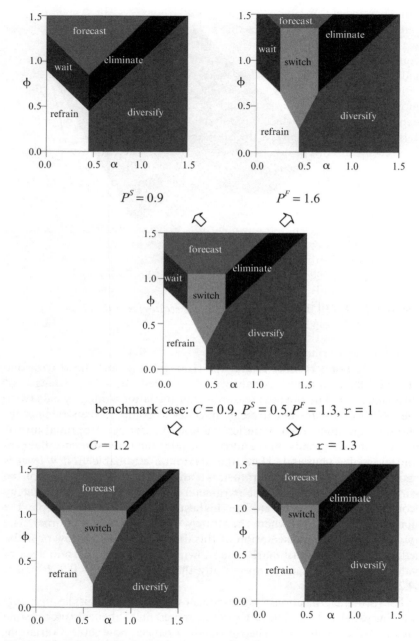

Figure 4.2   Optimal investment strategies with set-up costs

other parameters are left on their benchmark values. As before regions of the same shade indicate ranges of α and ϕ where a particular strategy generates the highest ENPV of all alternatives. The borders between any two regions consist of points where the level of ENPV under any two regimes is indifferent. Let us use the middle panel of Figure 4.2 to build intuition by first looking at two polar cases: in the case without uncertainty (that is, moving on the horizontal axis where $\phi = 0$), there is a critical level for the expected return above which it is optimal to start both projects immediately. It is that level of α that makes the ENPV positive. At lower levels of α neither project is realized. The other polar case is the one where the expected return as seen from period one is zero (that is, moving on the vertical axis where $\alpha = 0$). In this case there will always be just one, if any, project realized. Above a critical level of ϕ (the return on the better project in this case) it becomes optimal to wait in order to invest in the second period. Only when ϕ is sufficiently high does it become interesting to bear the forecasting costs and to start with the better project right away. In cases between the two polar situations outlined (that is, where $\alpha > 0$ and $\phi > 0$) the strategies of switching and eliminating become relevant. It is clear that the 45-degree line marks the border between diversification and eliminating: if the inferior project produces losses it will be discontinued in the second period.

The four peripheral panels of Figure 4.2 indicate the outcome of changing the benchmark conditions one at a time and leaving the remaining assumptions unchanged. Here, we mainly want to clarify how these parameters affect the choice of forecasting. The upper left-hand panel indicates that under the given initial parameter values an increase in switching costs to a value of 0.9 (that is, to the same level as C) altogether removes switching from the set of viable alternatives. Forecasting, as a result, becomes more widely applicable (as are waiting and eliminating). When the costs of forecasting are increased (viz. the upper right-hand panel where $PF = 1.6$) the reverse happens and forecasting is replaced either by waiting, switching or eliminating. Raising set-up costs (viz. the bottom left-hand panel where $C = 1.2$) favours forecasting at the cost of eliminating only. Raising the discount rate (viz. the bottom right-hand panel where $\rho = 1.3$) has no effect on forecasting. It only increases the range of parameters where none of the projects is ever operated. Under the present circumstances, this is the only effect a higher discount rate has.

4.2.2 Operating Costs

Here we analyse the investment decision when there are operating costs (V per period per project) but no fixed costs for setting up an operation. In this case the seven available strategies yield the following levels of ENPV:

1. Refraining: $\Pi = 0$

2. Going ahead: $\Pi = \alpha + \frac{\alpha}{\rho} - \frac{\rho + 1}{\rho} V$

3. Waiting: $\Pi = \frac{\alpha + \phi}{\rho} - \frac{1}{\rho} V$

4. Switching: $\Pi = \alpha + \frac{\alpha + \phi}{\rho} - \frac{\rho + 1}{\rho} V - \frac{1}{2} P^S$

5. Eliminating: $\Pi = 2\alpha + \frac{\alpha + \phi}{\rho} - \frac{2\rho + 1}{\rho} V$

6. Forecasting: $\Pi = \alpha + \phi + \frac{\alpha + \phi}{\rho} - \frac{\rho + 1}{\rho} V - P^F$

7. Diversifying: $\Pi = 2\left(\alpha + \frac{\alpha}{\rho} - \frac{\rho + 1}{\rho} V \right)$

The parameter values chosen for benchmark calculation are basically the same as in the previous case and with respect to operating costs $V = \frac{1}{2} C$ is chosen. This makes the costs of a project operated for two periods the same as before under fixed set-up costs. Given the numerical values used in the calculations the altered nature of costs only affects the ENPV of the strategies of waiting and eliminating. Nevertheless, the fact that one can save operating costs by not running (or by closing) an operation considerably changes the picture. First, the strategy of switching is now strictly dominated by either waiting or by eliminating.[4] However, the most important difference compared to the situation with set-up costs is that the strategies of waiting and eliminating replace diversification and forecasting over a wide range of α and ϕ values. The reason for this is simple: waiting as well as eliminating are cost-saving given costs are incurred only when a project is operated. Figure 4.3 again offers a three-dimensional visualization of the optimal strategy in relation to different levels of α and ϕ.

Turning to the last graphical display of this chapter, Figure 4.4 shows how varying parameter values under operating costs affect the choice of optimal strategy. Here, the display is limited to two panels: the left-hand panel presents the benchmark case. The right-hand panel shows the case with a higher level of operation costs. The results of the other parameter variations are left out because: (1) raising P^F to a level of 1.6 removes forecasting from the map; (2) raising P^S does not change the situation since

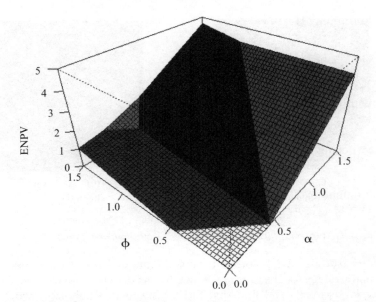

Figure 4.3   ENPV resulting from different strategies with operating costs

switching is not indicated even at the base rate of 0.5; and (3) with operating costs a change in the discount rate has no effect on strategy choice. Comparing the two benchmark cases in Figure 4.4 and in Figure 4.2 highlights the reduced importance of forecasting under operating costs. An increase in the level of operating costs (the left-hand panel of Figure 4.3 where $V = 0.6$) makes waiting dominate forecasting at low levels of α but in turn makes forecasting dominate eliminating at higher levels of α. This is because total operating costs are higher under eliminating than under forecasting, which in turn are higher than under waiting.

4.3   EFFECTS OF LOWERING FORECASTING COSTS

We start this section by noting that our two benchmark cases (with set-up costs and with operating costs) are based on a rather high level of forecasting costs. In fact, forecasting costs were set higher than the costs of actually operating a project for two periods. Comparing the two benchmark cases we find that forecasting, when expensive, is more widely used in the case with set-up costs than in the case with operating costs. How is the relevance of forecasting in the two cases affected as we consider lower levels

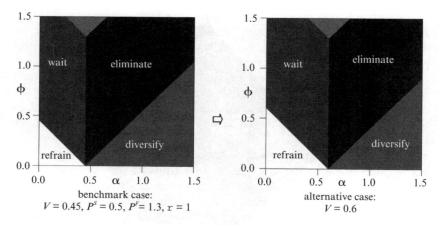

Figure 4.4   Optimal investment strategies with operating costs

of forecasting costs? In order to answer this question we compute the optimal strategy for the range of α and ϕ considered before with gradually lower levels of P^F and find that forecasting increasingly supersedes the other strategies. Notably, strategies where at least some projects are run for just one period (that is, waiting, eliminating and switching) are replaced first as forecasting becomes less expensive. Once P^F reaches a critical level (specific to each of the two cases) no other strategy but diversification is viable any longer. Also, as waiting, eliminating and switching become irrelevant, the difference between set-up costs and operating costs also becomes irrelevant. Overall, diversification proves to be the strategy most resistant to a reduction in forecasting costs.

4.4   SUMMARY AND FURTHER READING

We have seen here that forming expectations, when expensive, can be superseded by the possibility to wait, the strategy to switch projects, and the possibility to eliminate the inferior project. All these behavioural alternatives rely on letting the flow of time reveal information freely that, *ex ante*, would be available only at considerable cost. At low levels of forecasting costs, forecasting dominates these strategies which do not take advantage of the maximal duration of an investment project. Diversification over projects, however, remains a strategy that in many circumstances supersedes forecasting even at low costs of forecasting. The approach taken here of endogenizing the choice of risk strategy is so far rather unusual in economic analysis. In particular, an integrated analysis of strategies for dealing with uncertainty is largely missing in the management literature (see, for example, Armstrong, 2001, on forecasting techniques and Besanko et al., 2000, on diversification as a strategy option). The same holds for research on entrepreneurial information search (see Cooper et al., 2001).

Here, we have looked at optimal strategy choice in a relatively simple setting. In many economic situations the choice of the best strategy for dealing with an unknown future is difficult for the human decision maker. Chapter 6 will take up this theme by experimentally investigating whether subjects correctly assess the value of available information when forming expectations. The experimental evidence presented there indicates that many subjects fail to perceive the optimal strategy. Moreover, in reality there will often be fast and cheap forms of forecasting that are not optimal but are nevertheless useful. Hence, extrapolative expectations, the major form of such forecasting heuristics, will be introduced in the next chapter and will be further explored in Chapters 8 and 9.

NOTES

1. Alternatively, the forecast could merely reduce, instead of eliminate, uncertainty. In this case the forecaster would, for example, deliver information that would make one project the likely winner with probability γ where $\gamma > \frac{1}{2}$. With an imprecise forecast the ENPV under forecasting is smaller than in the set-up described above where $\gamma = 1$. Specifically, the ENPV in this more general case is

$$\Pi = \gamma\left(\alpha + \phi + \frac{\alpha + \phi}{\rho}\right) + (1 - \gamma)\left(\alpha + \frac{\alpha}{\rho}\right) - C - P^F.$$

   Clearly, the cost of forecasting may be a function of the precision of the forecast so that noisiness of the forecast just introduced does not necessarily make forecasting less desirable.
2. The nature of the firm's situation can be explained in terms of a game analogy: imagine a decision maker who can draw chips from either or both of two urns. He knows that in one of the urns there is a single chip of value $\alpha + \phi$ while the other urn contains a single chip of value $\alpha - \phi$ (take, for example, the values 4 and 2 implying $\alpha = 3$ and $\phi = 1$). If the decision maker chooses to become active in period one he makes a draw from one urn (the go-ahead strategy or the forecasting strategy) or from both urns (the diversification, switching or eliminating strategies). If the agent buys the forecasting service this means he is allowed to peek into the urns. Obviously, in this case he chooses the urn with the more valuable chip. With all other strategies the choice has to be done without looking into the urns. For period two the decision maker is allowed to see the contents of the urns at no cost. If the firm has waited for this information this is the moment to choose the chip of higher value. If the firm has made a pick in the first period the firm can either hold on to its choice (go-ahead strategy or diversify strategy), exchange chips (that is, switch) or give one chip back (that is, eliminate).
3. These parameters are chosen so as to have all six relevant strategies represented in the range of α and ϕ between 0 to 1.5. This is possible with the assumption that set-up costs are higher than switching costs and that forecasting costs are even higher than set-up costs.
4. When $\alpha > V - \frac{1}{2}P^s$, eliminating dominates switching and when $\alpha < V + \frac{1}{2}P^s$, waiting dominates switching.

5.   Expectations in time series models

5.1   INTRODUCTION

This chapter analyses expectations in a multi-period setting. This allows a dynamic analysis of expectations formation where economic facts and expectations co-evolve over time. We call the models presented here time series models in order to make a link with the statistical analysis of time series where this type of theoretical analysis has proved to be particularly fruitful. Important fields for applications of such models are, for example, agricultural and financial markets. The chapter begins with a definition of the conditional expectation of a random variable in a time series context. Based on this definition we clarify the notion of rational expectations and show under what conditions it is rational to use one of several specific forms of simple (heuristic) forecasting schemes. These expectations schemes are then introduced into a market model. We consider a situation where producers have to make input decisions one period before selling their output. This environment is familiar from agricultural production for which the first theoretical analyses of market dynamics were proposed. It is also the set-up that John Muth used in 1961 to introduce his concept of rational expectations and to explore the effects of different expectations schemes. The chapter then turns toward the study of stock price dynamics under different types of expectations formation. Here, we compare stock prices as determined by discounting of the total stream of future dividends with stock prices that result when market participants base their decisions on short-term expectations.

5.2   CONDITIONAL EXPECTATIONS IN TIME AND RATIONAL EXPECTATIONS

Consider a single producer for whom the pay-off of his efforts depends in part on a variable that is not under his control. For Robinson Crusoe this variable could, for example, be air temperature, rainfall or the tide level. For a more typical producer this variable could be the economy's total output. This exogenous variable shall be denoted by X and is assumed for concreteness to display persistence (measured by the coefficient η) over time, more concretely:

$$X_t = \xi + \eta X_{t-1} + \varepsilon_t^X, \text{ with } \xi > 0 \text{ and } 1 > \eta > 0. \tag{5.1}$$

This process is stationary and has a well-defined mean (or unconditional expected value) of $\mu_X = \xi/(1 - \eta)$. The autoregressive process that equation (5.1) characterizes means that above-average temperatures are more likely to be followed by above-average temperatures and below-average temperatures are more likely to be followed by below-average temperatures. The term ε_t^X is an identically, independently distributed random variable with a mean of zero. That is, the deviation of X_t from $\xi + \eta X_{t-1}$ cannot be predicted with any information available at time $t-1$. This makes the recent history of X the only helpful information for predicting the future of X. Consider now what happens when the output of the individual producer is a function of his input as well as a function of the described exogenous random variable X. For concreteness of the analysis we take the case where the amount of seeds invested now (S_t) leads to a harvest one period into the future (H_{t+1}) according to

$$H_{t+1} = \varphi X_{t+1} \ln S_t, \text{ where } \varphi > 0. \tag{5.2}$$

This stochastic production function displays diminishing marginal returns to the input of seeds. As of time t the producer (assumed risk neutral) maximizes his expected income in time $t + 1$, that is, the difference between expected output and input:

$$E_t(H_{t+1} - S_t) = \varphi E_t(X_{t+1}) \ln S_t - S_t. \tag{5.3}$$

Maximizing with respect to the input level yields:

$$S_t = \varphi E_t(X_{t+1}). \tag{5.4}$$

Clearly, the mathematical expectation of X is the decisive variable for input allocation here. The important point to note is that this expectation is a conditional expectation of X. It is the expectation of X_{t+1} given the information up to time t. Evidently, the producer decides on his input allocation with: (1) as much information as possible (all up to t); and (2) forms expectations one period ahead (that is, forecasting X for $t+1$ and not, for example, for $t+2$). If X follows the process indicated in (5.1) this conditional expectation is $E_t(X_{t+1}) = \xi + \eta X_t$. Hence, the rational producer decides period by period on his optimal input according to:

$$S_t = \varphi(\xi + \eta X_t). \tag{5.5}$$

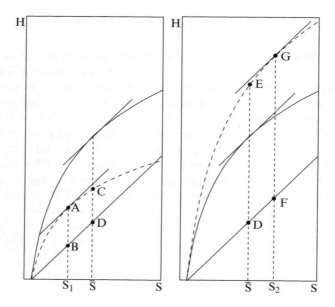

*Figure 5.1   Expected profit under below-average and above-average
                circumstances*

The time-dependent input allocation of (5.5) will (in expected terms) yield higher net profits than a constant input allocation based on an unconditional expectation of X. The unconditional expectation of X is simply the average level of X. The relevance of the conditional (or updated) expectation becomes clearer with the help of Figure 5.1. The solid curve in both panels of the figure displays as a benchmark the expected harvest if X is on its mean level $\xi/(1-\eta)$. The left-hand panel of Figure 5.1 shows a situation where X_t is actually below its mean. Hence, at any level of input, expected output for the next period is lower than in the benchmark case. If the producer allocates his inputs according to the conditional forecast of X (in this case expecting a below-average level of X) he chooses the below-average input level S_1 and realizes (in expected terms) a harvest level indicated by the distance between points A and B. Compare this to his harvest (in expected terms) if he were to allocate his inputs according to the unconditional forecast of X (that is, holding the input level fixed on its average level $\bar{S}$). Under the conditions of the left-hand panel the producer could in this case only hope to realize the distance between the points C and D. Clearly, this is less than the distance between A and B. The right-hand panel of Figure 5.1 shows the situation where X_t is above its mean. Again, in this case the producer who rightly chooses his (now higher than average) input level S_2 based on the conditional expectation of X realizes a higher expected harvest (measured by the distance between G and F) compared to a situation in which he would base his decision on an unconditional expectation of X where, with an input of $\overline{S}$, he could only hope to realize the profit according to the distance between E and D.

From the above it becomes clear that a particular expectation (or forecast) is rational when the value of the forecast is the mathematical expectation conditional on all relevant information (denoted by Inf_t) available at the time of decision. It is this projection that, when guiding input decisions, maximizes expected income. Hence, expectations are rational (denoted by the superscript *ra*) when:

$$X_{t+1}^{e,ra} = E(X_{t+1} \mid Inf_t). \tag{5.6}$$

In our example this means that only the following type of expectation is rational:

$$X_{t+1}^{e,ra} = E(X_{t+1} \mid X_t) = \xi + \eta X_t. \tag{5.7}$$

Note that making a forecast like (5.7) means that the decision maker needs to know the values of the parameters ξ and η. This implies that the decision maker or somebody who assists him has to estimate these parameters from historical data. For the moment we assume that information is free and the costs of developing and estimating statistical models are negligible. We will return to this issue but for now we simply list several other forms (schemes) of expectations:

- Static expectations: $X_{t+1}^{e,st} = X_t$
- Adaptive expectations:[1] $X_{t+1}^{e,ad} = X_t^{e,ad} + \lambda(X_t - X_t^{e,ad})$
- Level-extrapolative expectations: $X_{t+1}^{e,l-e} = \omega_0 + \omega_1 X_t$
- Trend-extrapolative expectations: $X_{t+1}^{e,t-e} = X_t + \Omega(X_t - X_{t-1})$
- Regressive expectations: $X_{t+1}^{e,reg} = X_t - \tau(X_t - \mu)$.
- Multivariate expectations $X_{t+1}^{e,mv} = \vartheta_0 + \vartheta_1 X_t + \vartheta_2 L_t$.

Here λ, ω_0, ω_1, Ω, τ, μ, ϑ_0, ϑ_1 and ϑ_2 are behavioural parameters that can differ from agent to agent and L_t stands for possible relevant variables. The first five expectations schemes are univariate in nature and rely only on the history of the variable to be forecasted. The last type of expectations scheme in the list is of the multivariate type. Clearly, for many of these expectations schemes there exists a more elaborate version.

Applying the definition of rational forecasts in a context as described by (5.1) and (5.2) makes the level-extrapolative form of expectations with the specific parameters $\omega_0 = \xi$ and $\omega_1 = \eta$ the rational form of expectations. However, in a different context another expectations scheme may be the rational one to adopt. Going through the list of expectations schemes above we can describe the conditions under which each scheme is the rational forecast:

- Static expectations are rational if X follows a random walk
  $X_t = X_{t-1} + \varepsilon_t^X$.
- Adaptive expectations are rational if X follows
  $X_t = X_{t-1} - (1 - \lambda)\varepsilon_{t-1}^X + \varepsilon_t^X$.[2]
- Level-extrapolative expectations are rational if X follows
  $X_t = \omega_0 + \omega_1 X_{t-1} + \varepsilon_t^X$.
- Trend-extrapolative expectations are rational if X follows
  $\Delta X_t \equiv X_t - X_{t-1} = \Omega \Delta X_{t-1} + \varepsilon_t^X$.
- Regressive expectations are rational if X follows
  $X_t = \mu\tau + (1 - \tau)X_{t-1} + \varepsilon_t^X$.
- Multivariate expectations are rational if X follows
  $X_t = \vartheta_0 + \vartheta_1 X_{t-1} + \vartheta_2 L_{t-1} + \varepsilon_t^X$.

Hence, for any of the described expectations schemes there exists an environment to which it offers the rational forecast. We now return to the issue of costs of forming expectations and note that in reality agents use (or their behaviour accords to) one or another of these schemes because they are cheaper than a rational forecast. Think, for example, about static expectations (that is, status quo expectations) which are available without any computations at all. Hence, the above list with the different forms of expectations can be seen as a list of heuristics that people adopt even when these expectations are not fully optimal. Heuristics are rules of thumb or shortcuts that according to researchers are widely used by decision makers because by and large they lead to good choices while saving time and mental effort (see Todd, 2001). Following Simon (1972) we call expectations based on one of these schemes 'boundedly rational' except when the particular scheme under the current circumstances is the optimal scheme. The important economic questions that follow from this are: (1) how do markets perform when agents use heuristic expectations schemes? And (2) how do market outcomes under heuristic expectations compare to outcomes under rational expectations?

5.3 A MARKET MODEL WITH STATIC, ADAPTIVE AND RATIONAL EXPECTATIONS

5.3.1 Static and Adaptive Expectations

The model introduced here has a long tradition in dynamic economic analysis. Early studies were provided by Ezekiel (1938) and Buchanan (1939). The subject of this analysis is the cyclical pattern of output and prices in markets for products with significant production lag. The so-called 'hog cycle' has been known to business people for a long time and entered the economic journal literature in the 1920s (see Sarle, 1925). Consider the supply function:

$$s_t = \gamma p_t^e + u_t, \text{ with } u_t = \rho u_{t-1} + \varepsilon_t \text{ and } 1 \geq \rho \geq 0, \tag{5.8}$$

where variables are understood to be deviations from long-run equilibrium values.[3] Appendix 5.1 shows how the supply function is derived from expected profit maximization of producers. For concreteness we look at two special cases. When the parameter ρ is zero, output shocks (that is, unpredictable deviations of output from plan) are transitory. The other case is the one where shocks to output are persistent. This is the case where $\rho = 1$. A world with this type of shock is a world in which, for example, unpredictable changes to available technology and to economic institutions affect output permanently. Figure 5.2 shows the dynamics of u_t after a one-time shock in the two cases discussed.

The demand for the good by consumers is captured by:

$$d_t = -\beta p_t. \tag{5.9}$$

The market is assumed to always be in equilibrium.[4] Hence:

$$d_t = s_t. \tag{5.10}$$

This allows the determination of the equilibrium price:

$$p_t = -\frac{\gamma}{\beta} p_t^e - \frac{1}{\beta} u_t. \tag{5.11}$$

In order to solve the model we need to specify the price expectations (that is, p_t^e) of producers. The simplest form of expectations considered here are static expectations, that is, $p_t^e = p_{t-1}$. In this case the market price evolves according to:[5]

$$p_t = -\frac{\gamma}{\beta} p_{t-1} - \frac{1}{\beta} u_t. \tag{5.12}$$

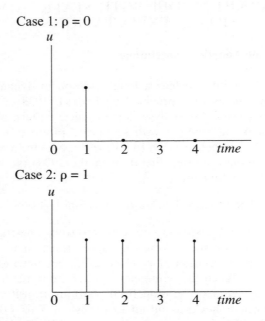

*Figure 5.2   The dynamics of u_t after a one-time shock to output in
period one*

If $\beta > \gamma$, that is, if the slope of the demand curve is larger in absolute terms
than the slope of the supply curve, then the price path after a disruption of
the long-run equilibrium is oscillatory yet stable. Consider as an alternative
expectations scheme the adaptive form. Here we have:

$$p_t^e - p_{t-1}^e = \lambda(p_{t-1} - p_{t-1}^e). \tag{5.13}$$

If we solve (5.11) for p_t^e and insert this into (5.13) we find:

$$p_t = \left(1 - \lambda - \frac{\lambda\gamma}{\beta}\right)p_{t-1} - \frac{1}{\beta}u_t + \frac{1-\lambda}{\beta}u_{t-1}. \tag{5.14}$$

Hence, with the change from static to adaptive expectations the dynamics
of price adjustment change. It is still possible that there are oscillatory
dynamics but it is also possible that the dynamic adjustment of the market
price is monotonous. The critical value for the occurrence of the latter form
of dynamic adjustment is $\lambda < \beta/(\beta + \gamma)$.

5.3.2 Market Dynamics under Rational Expectations

We now want to investigate how the agricultural market functions when expectations, instead of following one of the expectations heuristics (like static expectations), are fully rational. As indicated before this means that expectations of economic decision makers must coincide with the mathematical expectations of the variable forecast. In a market model the application of this concept (that is, of equation 5.6) becomes more complicated than in the simple production optimization problem treated earlier in this chapter. In a market context, the concept of rational expectations demands of market participants that they fully understand the market mechanism. This is often described by stating that under rational expectations agents are assumed to know the model of the world in which they live and operate. This concept of rational expectations was introduced by Muth (1961). Analytically, rational price expectations in our model can be expressed as:

$$p_t^{e,ra} = E[p_t | Inf_{t-1}] = E_{t-1}(p_t). \qquad (5.15)$$

Here Inf_{t-1} denotes all relevant information at time $t-1$. Specifically, this information consists: (1) of the behavioural relationships determining the functioning of the market (that is, equations 5.8, 5.9 and 5.10); and (2) of values of the relevant variables at time $t-1$. In the concrete case at hand, under the hypothesis that producers form rational expectations, the model is solved in two steps: first, equation (5.15) is inserted into equation (5.11) to yield:

$$p_t = -\frac{\gamma}{\beta}E_{t-1}(p_t) - \frac{1}{\beta}u_t. \qquad (5.16)$$

Second, taking mathematical expectations of both sides of equation (5.16) we find:[6]

$$E_{t-1}(p_t) = -\frac{\gamma}{\beta}E_{t-1}[E_{t-1}(p_t)] - \frac{1}{\beta}E_{t-1}(u_t) \qquad (5.17)$$

Since the mathematical expectation of the mathematical expectation of a variable is nothing but the mathematical expectation of that variable (this is called the law of iterated expectations), we can solve (5.17) for the rational price expectation:

$$E_{t-1}(p_t) = -\frac{\rho}{\beta + \gamma}u_{t-1}. \qquad (5.18)$$

Inserting this expression into (5.16) yields the solution for the market price under rational expectations:

$$p_t = -\frac{\rho}{\beta + \gamma}u_{t-1} - \frac{1}{\beta}\varepsilon_t \qquad (5.19)$$

The first thing to note is that in this market environment with rational expectations there is never an issue of stability. Unlike the cases of static and adaptive expectations the lagged price does not affect the current price and there are neither (deterministic) oscillations nor is there any room for divergent dynamics.[7] Next, we look at the two polar cases introduced (that is, $\rho = 0$ and $\rho = 1$). In the first case the price determined in a market with rational producers simply fluctuates randomly around its constant long-run equilibrium value. In the second case the price reaches its new long-run equilibrium level in the period right after a (permanent) supply shock has occurred.

It is interesting to note that in the context of the model presented here and depending on the value for ρ, adaptive or regressive expectations may in fact be rational. Consider first the case with $\rho = 1$: if the adjustment parameter of adaptive expectations λ is exactly $\beta/(\beta + \gamma)$ then equation (5.14) reduces to (5.19) which is the expression describing price dynamics under rational expectations. Hence, for a world with permanent supply shocks adaptive expectations with just the right adjustment parameter leads to the same market outcome as under rational expectations. If in the case with $\rho = 0$ expectations are formed regressively with the adjustment parameter $\tau = -1$ and with the anchor parameter $\mu = 0$, then an equation similar to (5.14) reduces to (5.19) which, in this setting, is the expression for the market price under rational expectations. Thus, in a situation with only temporary shocks regressive expectations can yield the same outcome as under rational expectations. These two cases illustrate the fact that if producers choose the appropriate extrapolative scheme the market will function as if its producers formed rational expectations.

5.3.3   Heterogeneous Expectations

What happens when different types of producers interact on the market? The most interesting case is the one when some producers form rational expectations and the other producers form heuristic (that is, boundedly rational) expectations. For concreteness we analyse a set-up with a mix of Muthian rational producers and producers who form static expectations. It is important to note that in this case the behaviour of the rational types will be affected by the presence of the boundedly rational types. Keeping with the set-up already introduced, the supply function under heterogeneous expectations is:

$$s_t = \chi\gamma E_{t-1}(p_t) + (1 - \chi)\gamma p_{t-1} + u_t. \tag{5.20}$$

Here, the parameter χ indicates the fraction of rational agents. Inserting this equation into the market-clearing condition, and going through the same steps outlined in the last section for solving for the mathematical expectation of the price, the following price equation results:

$$p_t = -\frac{(1 - \chi)\gamma}{\beta + \chi\gamma} p_{t-1} - \frac{\chi\gamma\rho}{\beta(\beta + \chi\gamma)} u_{t-1} - \frac{1}{\beta} u_t. \tag{5.21}$$

Clearly, this solution simplifies to (5.12) for the case of static expectations (that is, with $\chi = 0$) and to (5.19) for the case of homogeneous rational expectations (that is, with $\chi = 1$). Intuition regarding the influence of rational actors can be built by considering the special case with $\rho = 0$. For this case the price equation is:

$$p_t = -\frac{(1 - \chi)\gamma}{\beta + \chi\gamma} p_{t-1} - \frac{1}{\beta} u_t. \tag{5.22}$$

From the coefficient of the lagged price term it becomes apparent that increasing the fraction of rational players reduces autocorrelation of the market price more than proportionally. For a numerical example take $\gamma = 1$ and $\beta = 2$. In this case the coefficient on the lagged price is -0.5 in a situation where all producers (homogeneously) form static expectations. With 50 per cent of rational producers this coefficient is changed to -0.2 and not just to -0.25 as a casual analysis might suggest. Rational producers tend to exploit the opportunities offered by the non-rational producers. Specifically, in times of high (low) prices rational producers tend to reduce (increase) planned output because they correctly anticipate the imminent price fall (rise).

5.3.4 Comparison of Price Dynamics under Different Expectations

It is instructive to assess the difference in price dynamics under different expectations schemes of producers by way of simulations. This is done here by means of two scenarios. In both scenarios we use the same parameters $\rho = 1$ and $\gamma = 1$. Scenario one further assumes $\beta = 1.1$ while scenario two assumes a more price elastic demand with $\beta = 2$. The disturbance ε_t is randomly drawn (by the computer) from a normal distribution with a mean of zero and a standard deviation of one. Figure 5.3 shows the resulting price dynamics for the cases of static, adaptive and rational expectations. Panel a) shows the simulated price for 30 periods under scenario one and panel b) shows prices under scenario two.

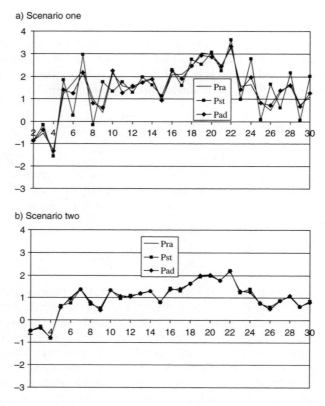

*Figure 5.3   Price dynamics with different expectations schemes of
               producers*

The adjustment parameter for adaptive expectations (λ) in the two scenarios is chosen to lie midway between one (the level for static expectations)
and the level $\beta/(\beta + \gamma)$ that makes adaptive expectations equivalent to rational expectations. The simulations show that in the present set-up with adaptive expectations prices move close to the rational expectations outcome.
Moreover, it is apparent from a comparison of the two scenarios that the
strong cycling of prices, particularly under static expectations, and the resulting deviations from the rational expectations outcome depends on the relative size of the slopes of market demand and market supply functions: with
a relatively price-elastic market demand (that is, in scenario two) prices under
different expectations schemes deviate less from each other than under a
price-inelastic market demand. Hence, it becomes clear that deviations from
rationality in expectations do not necessarily generate sizable market effects.

5.4   EXPECTATIONS AND STOCK PRICES

We now turn to a different type of market, and deal with the role of expectations of investors on financial markets. The stock market is widely seen as one of the most important markets in a capitalist society. By valuing enterprises the stock market determines the amount of resources a firm (or the business sector as a whole) is allocated. The model for the valuation of a firm's stock outlined here takes the (gross) interest rate (I) on risk-free bonds as given. The risk premium θ (the difference between the expected return on this stock and the risk-free interest rate) is also given.[8] The 'efficient valuation' of a stock is commonly understood to be that price that equals the net present value of all rationally expected future dividends paid to the holder of the stock evaluated at the risk-adjusted discount rate (that is, $R \equiv I + \theta$). This is called the 'rational expectations fundamental value' of the stock (P_t^{rafu}). Formally, this is:

$$P_t^{rafu} = E_t\left(\sum_{l=1}^{\infty} \frac{Z_{t+l}}{R^l}\right). \tag{5.23}$$

In order to illustrate how P^{rafu} is computed we look at a concrete case where the firm's dividends follow a first-order autoregressive process:

$$Z_t = \alpha_0 + \alpha_1 Z_{t-1} + \varepsilon_t^Z, \text{ with } \alpha_0 \geq 0 \text{ and } 0 < \alpha_1 \leq 1. \tag{5.24}$$

Appendix 5.2 details how to calculate the rational expectations fundamental value according to (5.23) when dividends follow the process given in (5.24). The result of these calculations is:

$$P_t^{rafu} = \frac{\alpha_0 R}{(R-1)(R-\alpha_1)} + \frac{\alpha_1}{R-\alpha_1} Z_t. \tag{5.25}$$

This stock price resulting from an efficient functioning of the market will serve as a benchmark in the remaining discussion of this chapter.[9]

5.4.1   Non-rational Dividend Expectations

Here, we contrast the rational expectations fundamental valuation of stocks just outlined with the valuation that results when agents – while still discounting future dividends – form static dividend expectations instead of rational expectations. In this case the expected dividend for any horizon is the current dividend payment. Hence, the resulting stock price that results when agents discount future dividends and apply static expectations is:

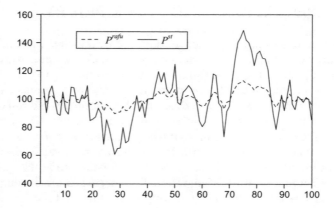

*Figure 5.4   The stock price with static and rational dividend expectations
with long-term discounting*

$$P_t^{st} = \left(\sum_{l=1}^{\infty} \frac{Z_t}{R^l} \right) = \frac{Z_t}{R-1}. \tag{5.26}$$

Clearly, as noted before in the special case where dividends follow a
random walk (that is, if $\alpha_0 = 0$ and $\alpha_1 = 1$) static expectations of dividends
are rational and (5.25) reduces to (5.26). However, if for example dividends
follow a process with $\alpha_1 < 1$ (that is, a stationary AR1-process) agents
forming static expectation would not value the stock efficiently. As an
example we look at a situation where $\alpha_0 = 2$, $\alpha_1 = 0.8$ and where ε_t^Z is normally distributed with a mean of zero and a standard deviation of one. For
our stochastic simulations we use a value for R of 1.1. Figure 5.4 shows the
time paths for P^{rafu} and P^{st}. The path of the stock price under static dividend
expectations in this case shows substantial deviations from the efficient valuation under rational expectations. These deviations can be positive as well
as negative, and they can last for several periods. In the simulated market
there are three sub-samples of ten or more periods where P_t^{st} lies above or
below P^{rafu}. The course of the simulated P^{st}-series very much resembles the
overreaction of actual stock prices relative to rationally valued *ex post* dividends as reported by Shiller (1981). Hence, non-rational dividend expectations are one candidate for excessive volatility of stock prices.

5.4.2   Short-Term Expectations

In this subsection we investigate stock price determination when agents: (1)
only look one period into the future and form expectations of next period's

dividend and next period's price; and (2) shift funds into (or out of) stocks as long as the expected return on stocks over one period exceeds (of falls short of) the risk-adjusted return on bonds. Under these circumstances and with homogenous investors the stock price will be in equilibrium when it satisfies the following condition:

$$P_t = \frac{P^e_{t+1} + Z^e_{t+1}}{R}. \tag{5.27}$$

Hence, under this behavioural assumption the stock price is the value of next period's expected price plus next period's expected dividend discounted by R. When agents form static expectations both for the dividend and the stock price (5.27) simplifies to:

$$P^{sdsp}_t = \frac{Z_t}{R-1}. \tag{5.28}$$

Here, the superscript *sdsp* stands for static expectations for dividends and static expectations for the price. The market price in (5.28) is exactly the same stock price as determined in (5.26). Hence, static dividend expectations in combination with static price expectations determine the same market price as static dividend expectations in conjunction with long-term dividend discounting. In this specific case there is no separate effect of price expectations on the stock price. However, this result does not hold for other forms of price expectations. Consider as an illustration (a form of) trend-extrapolative price expectations, that is, trend-reversing expectations:

$$P^{e,t-e}_{t+1} = P_t + \Omega(P_t - P_{t-1}) \text{ with } \Omega < 0, \tag{5.29}$$

in combination with static dividend expectations. This determines the equilibrium stock price:

$$P^{sdtp}_t = \frac{Z_t - \Omega P^{sdtp}_{t-1}}{R-1-\Omega}, \tag{5.30}$$

where the superscript *sdtp* stands for static dividend and trend-reversing price expectations. Figure 5.5 shows the stock price for a specific parameterization of this case where $\Omega = -0.5$ together with the stock price under static expectations derived before.[10] In this particular case, trend-reversing price expectations have the tendency to smooth stock price fluctuations.

Next, we want to show that even when only short-term expectations are relevant the resulting stock valuation may be efficient. For this purpose we inquire what expectation of next period's stock price (as a function of observable variables) together with a rational one-period-ahead dividend

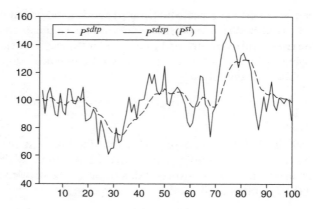

Figure 5.5   *The stock price with static and trend-reversing price*
expectations

forecast guarantees that short-term arbitrageurs determine a stock price
equal to the rational expectations' fundamental value. The answer to this
question is found in two steps: (1) we have to conjecture a functional form
for the relationship between currently observed relevant variables and the
equilibrium market price; and (2) we have to form rational one-period-
ahead forecasts. A simple (and promising) form of a price–dividend conjecture is:

$$P_t^{ra} = \phi_0 + \phi_1 Z_t, \tag{5.31}$$

where ϕ_0 and ϕ_1 are parameters yet to be determined and the superscript
ra stands for a market price under rational expectations.[11] The rational one-
period-ahead forecast (expectation) of dividends on the basis of (5.24) is:

$$E_t(Z_{t+1}) = \alpha_0 + \alpha_1 Z_t. \tag{5.32}$$

Combine (5.31) with (5.32) to find (as an intermediate step) the price forecast for the next period:

$$E_t(P_{t+1}^{ra}) = \phi_0 + \phi_1 \alpha_0 + \phi_1 \alpha_1 Z_t. \tag{5.33}$$

When the mathematical expectation for dividend payments and for the
stock price in the next period (that is, 5.32 and 5.33) are inserted into (5.27)
we find after collecting terms:

$$\phi_0 R + \phi_1 R Z_t = (\phi_0 + \alpha_0 + \phi_1 \alpha_0) + \alpha_1 (\phi_1 + 1) Z_t. \tag{5.34}$$

The equality of the left-hand side and the right-hand side is only guaranteed for all values of Z if the intercept terms and the slope terms on either side of (5.34) are identical. This means:

$$\phi_0 R = (\phi_0 + \alpha_0 + \phi_1 \alpha_0) \text{ and } \phi_1 R = \alpha_1 (\phi_1 + 1), \qquad (5.35)$$

respectively. This implies that ϕ_0 and ϕ_1 are now determined:

$$\phi_0 = \frac{\alpha_0 R}{(R-1)(R-\alpha_1)} \text{ and } \phi_1 = \frac{\alpha_1}{R-\alpha_1} \qquad (5.36)$$

The equilibrium price under rational expectations is thus determined by inserting these solutions for ϕ_0 and ϕ_1 into equation (5.3):

$$P_t^{ra} = \frac{\alpha_0 R}{(R-1)(R-\alpha_1)} + \frac{\alpha_1}{R-\alpha_1} Z_t \qquad (5.37)$$

This solution is identical to the rational expectations fundamental solution in (5.25). Hence, the price forecast of (5.33) is the one that generates the rational expectations fundamental solution when market participants' behaviour is guided by short-term expectations. For one thing this shows when short-term expectations are consistent with efficient valuation of stocks, and it also concludes the description of one solution for the equilibrium price under rational expectations. Interestingly, (5.37) is not the only possible rational expectations solution. There are other (in fact an infinite number of) price conjectures that lead to market price dynamics that are consistent with that price conjecture. Consider the following case (the so-called 'bubble' case) where the price conjecture (5.31) is augmented by a term B (for bubble):

$$P_t = \phi_0 + \phi_1 Z_t + B_t. \qquad (5.38)$$

If we apply the same solution method just introduced we find the condition:

$$\phi_0 R + \phi_1 R Z_t + R B_t = (\phi_0 + \alpha_0 + \phi_1 \alpha_0) + \alpha_1(\phi_1 + 1)Z_t + E_t(B_{t+1}). \quad (5.39)$$

For the paramaters ϕ_0 and ϕ_1 this condition leads to the same values as before. However, there is as the further condition:

$$E_t(B_{t+1}) = R B_t. \qquad (5.40)$$

This means that B_t must follow:

$$B_t = R B_{t-1} + \varepsilon_t^B, \qquad (5.41)$$

where ε_t^B is a random variable with a mean of zero. Hence, we can express this rational expectations solution as:

$$P_t^{ra} = P_t^{rafu} + B_t, \tag{5.42}$$

where B_t must be expected to grow exponentially. This is called the rational expectations bubble solution.[12] Intuitively, (5.42) means that the stock price can deviate from the rational expectations fundamental value without rational agents selling the stock as long as the deviation (B_t, the bubble) is expected to grow exponentially. The expected (and realized) capital gain is then just large enough to justify the overvaluation of the stock relative to the present value of rationally expected dividends.[13]

5.5   EMPIRICAL ASSESSMENT OF EXPECTATIONS HYPOTHESES

In later chapters of this book we will conduct tests of the hypothesis of rationality of foresight in various experimental settings. At this point, for assessing the model variants surveyed in this chapter it is helpful to present a brief survey of empirical research on expectations formation. A good introductory text is Holden et al. (1985). Early tests of various expectations hypotheses were typically conducted with survey data. This sort of study relies on data gathered from producers or consumers over many years. Individual forecasts can then be held against actual outcomes. Many of the studies in this tradition, like Figlewski and Wachtel (1981), Lovell (1986), Zellner (1986) and Pesaran (1987), reject the notion of rational expectations. In the wake of these critical results researchers have inspected the validity of these findings on statistical grounds: Jeong and Maddala (1991), Smyth (1992) and Lee (1994) explicitly address possible measurement errors in survey data and nevertheless reject rationality in most cases. The problem of aggregation bias in rationality tests has been analysed by Keane and Runkle (1990) and Bonham and Cohen (1995). These two studies suggest that the hypothesis of rationality is still rejected when adequate statistical procedures are used. When tests on the basis of survey data show stark deviations from rational expectations, these results may be artifacts arising because: (1) agents – in particular organizations as opposed to individuals – use forecasts that are better than those delivered to the surveying institutions; and (2) strong biases can arise because agents have to report qualitative answers in surveys (see Rötheli, 1999, 2005).

Experimental analyses (see Fisher, 1962; Schmalensee, 1976, for early exploratory studies) either ask subjects for an assessment of the course of an experimentally controlled variable or enact a market process with many subjects. In the first type of experiment (see, for example, Williams, 1987; Bolle, 1988a, 1988b; Hey, 1994) rationality of expectations can be tested independently of other hypotheses. While the results of these tests are not uncontroversial (see Dwyer et al., 1993) the rational expectations hypothesis is mostly rejected in these studies. In the second setting the rational expectations hypothesis is tested alongside other hypotheses (for example, of market clearing). Many studies of this type indicate that rational expectations are not empirically supported (see, for example, Smith et al., 1988; Porter and Smith, 2003; but see Plott and Sunder, 1988, for some support for the rational expectations hypothesis).

Besides the research strategies outlined above there exist a vast number of econometric studies of various markets relying on historical data (without using measures of expectations such as surveys) that investigate expectations hypotheses. Just concentrating on agricultural and financial markets – the two markets covered in this chapter – there is much critical evidence concerning rationality of expectations in the sense proposed by Muth. For applications to agricultural markets Nerlove and Fornari (1998) document the state of the art of testing rational expectation. For financial markets Shiller (1981), De Bondt and Thaler (1985), Chow (1989), Kelly (1997) and Cohen et al. (2005) offer econometric analyses rejecting rationality of foresight.

To sum up, many detailed empirical studies on expectations formation suggest that expectations are not formed rationally in the sense proposed by Muth (1961). Instead, economic agents widely use one or another form of extrapolative (possibly adaptive) expectations. See, for example, Nerlove (1983), Lovell (1986), Pesaran (1987), Williams (1987), Levine (1993) and Rötheli (1999) for details.[14]

5.6   SUMMARY AND FURTHER READING

This chapter gives only a short presentation of many interesting issues in time series models with expectations. It particularly focuses on price dynamics under various forms of expectations heuristics and under rational expectations. It also clarifies the role of the expectations horizon for the determination of prices, particularly of stock prices. There are many important issues that the interested reader can find in the literature of the last several decades. Blanchard and Fischer (1989), Cuthbertson (1996), Turnovsky (2000) and LeRoy (2004) offer informative presentations and extensions on the subject of speculative bubbles and related concepts. The studies presented in Gardes and Prat (2000) analyse the role of expectations in a variety of markets. Evans and Honkapohja (2001) provide a detailed analysis of the issue of learning in models as, for example, the one described in section 5.3. Wenzelburger (2004) and Pötzelberger and Sögner (2004) explore issues of learning in asset market models. Guesnerie (2001) explores the issue of multiple equilibria in rational expectation models and its potential for a theory of endogenous fluctuations based on so-called sunspot equilibria (see also Duffy and Fisher, 2005, for experimental evidence). The role of expectations heuristics will be further investigated in Chapters 8 and 9 of this book where we address expectations based on simple visual patterns in time series.

NOTES

1. $X_t^{e,ad}$ stands for the expectations for time t formed in time $t-1$.
2. This is a moving average process of order one with drift. The potential optimality of adaptive expectations under this condition was first noted by Muth (1960).
3. That is $s_t = (S_t - \overline{S})$ and $p_t^e = (P_t^e - \overline{P})$.
4. Turnovsky (1983) explores how price dynamics in such a market are affected if in addition to the spot market there is a futures market and speculators' demand for the good becomes relevant.
5. Given the condition of market clearing, the quantity produced (q_t) can always be expressed as $-\beta p_t$.
6. The two rules for mathematical expectations relevant here are: (1) the expected value of a sum is the sum of the expected values of its parts; (2) the expected value of a product of a constant and a random variable is the product of the constant and the expected value of the random variable.
7. See section 5.4.2 for a discussion of divergent price dynamics under rational expectations.
8. The key determinants of the risk premium are the variance of stock returns and the risk aversion of investors.
9. Consider the possibility that the firm may go out of business in the future. The simplest form of modelling this is to have a survival probability ψ. Hence, at any point in time next period's dividend is paid out according to (5.24) with probability ψ and with probability $(1 - \psi)$ no more dividends are paid out at any future date. It turns out that with the possibility of default the rational expectations fundamental value is simply altered to have a higher (that is, default risk-adjusted) discount rate $R^* = R/\psi$ instead of R.
10. In fact, $\Omega \leq 0$ is necessary for stability here.
11. See McCallum (1989) for a good presentation and many applications of the method of undetermined coefficients.
12. B_t could, in principle, be negative. In this case the undervaluation of the stock relative to the rational expectations fundamental value is justified with the expected capital loss. However, in this case foresight would strictly need to be short-sighted. With a longer horizon market participants would foresee the lower bound of zero for the stock price and by way of backward induction would conclude that the stock was undervalued and thus drive its price to P_t^{rafu}.
13. There are many extensions and qualifications to the bubble concept; see the chapter summary for further reading.
14. In many sorts of applications economic researchers continue to use rational expectations. A hypothesis like rational expectations (despite its limited realism) may be fruitful for empirical research because it is a parsimonious way of modelling expectations. This

is particularly relevant when the study of a phenomenon involves various other economic hypotheses. In such circumstances a hypothesis like rational expectations helps to reduce the number of parameters that need to be estimated. Also, it is a legitimate and potentially fruitful endeavour – paralleling the analysis in Chapter 4 – to explain observed deviations from one model of rationality (like Muth's) as the outcome of a rational strategy. In this respect various models of learning (see, for example, Caskey, 1985, and Brock and Hommes, 1997) and analyses of rational differentiation of expectations (for example, Branch, 2004) have been proposed.

APPENDIX 5.1   THE SUPPLY FUNCTION DERIVED FROM EXPECTED PROFIT MAXIMIZATION

The representative (risk-neutral) producer maximizes his expected profit by setting the appropriate input level K_0:

$$Max\ E_0(\Pi_1) = E_0[P_1 Q_1 - C_1(K_0)]$$

Here, Π stands for profit, P is market price, Q is quantity produced, K is input (for example, capital) and C are costs. The time subscripts are 0 indicating time of the production decision and 1 indicating the time of sales (harvest).

The optimality condition is:

$$\frac{\partial E_0(\Pi_1)}{\partial K_0} = \frac{\partial E_0(P_1 Q_1)}{\partial K_0} - \frac{\partial E_0[C_1(K_0)]}{\partial K_0} = 0$$

Further assumptions:

(a) $E_0(P_1 Q_1) = E_0(P_1)E_0(Q_1) + \sigma_{P_1 Q_1} = E_0(P_1)E_0(Q_1),$

since the market price is uncorrelated with the output of an individual producer in an atomistic market.

(b) The production function is $Q_1 = K_0 + u_1$, where u_1 is a shock with the characteristic $E_0(u_1) = 0$.
Hence, $E_0(Q_1) = K_0$ and, together with point (a) above, $\dfrac{\partial E_0(P_1 Q_1)}{\partial K_0} = E_0(P_1)$.

(c) $E_0[C_1(K_0)] = C(K_0),$

since costs are all incurred in period zero and are known with certainty (that is, no cost uncertainty). For simplicity:

$$C(K_0) = aK_0 + 0.5bK_0^2, \text{ implying} \frac{\partial E_0[C_1(K_0)]}{\partial K_0} = a + bK_0.$$

Hence, the optimality condition is $E_0(P_1) - a - bK_0 = 0$, and optimal input is $K_0 = -(a/b) + (1/b)E_0(P_1)$. Thus, the quantity actually produced by the individual producer is $Q_1 = -(a/b) + (1/b)E_0(P_1) + u_1$. With n identical individual producers the aggregate market supply is thus $Q_1^{aggregate} = -(na/b) + (n/b)E_0(P_1) + nu_1$.

APPENDIX 5.2 COMPUTATION OF THE RATIONAL EXPECTATIONS FUNDAMENTAL PRICE

The starting point here is equation (5.23):

$$P_t^{rafu} = E_t\left(\sum_{l=1}^{\infty} \frac{Z_{t+l}}{R^l}\right)$$

This can be rewritten as:

$$P_t^{rafu} = \sum_{l=1}^{\infty} \frac{E_t Z_{t+l}}{R^l}.$$

Remember that the process for dividends according to (5.25) is:

$$Z_t = \alpha_0 + \alpha_1 Z_{t-1} + \varepsilon_t^Z, \text{ with } 0 < \alpha_1 < 0.$$

The rationally expected dividend in the next period is:

$$E_t Z_{t+1} = \alpha_0 + \alpha_1 Z_t$$

The rationally expected dividend two periods into the future is:

$$E_t Z_{t+2} = \alpha_0 + \alpha_1 E_t Z_{t+1} = \alpha_0 + \alpha_0 \alpha_1 + \alpha_1^2 Z_t$$

Accordingly, the rationally expected dividend l periods into the future is:

$$E_t Z_{t+l} = \sum_{i=1}^{l} \alpha_0 \alpha_1^{i-1} + \alpha_1^l Z_t$$

Hence, equation (5.23) can be written as:

$$P_t^{rafu} = \sum_{l=1}^{\infty} \frac{E_t Z_{t+l}}{R^l} = \underbrace{\sum_{l=1}^{\infty} \frac{\overbrace{\sum_{i=1}^{l} \alpha_0 \alpha_1^{i-1}}^{A}}{R^l}}_{B} + \underbrace{\sum_{l=1}^{\infty} \left(\frac{\alpha_1}{R}\right)^l Z_t}_{C}.$$

This expression is evaluated in several steps. First, the sum of the infinite series denoted by A is assessed:

$$A = \alpha_0 + \alpha_0 \alpha_1 + \alpha_0 \alpha_1^2 + \ldots + \alpha_0 \alpha_1^{l-1}$$
$$\alpha_1 A = \alpha_0 \alpha_1 + \alpha_0 \alpha_1^2 + \alpha_0 \alpha_1^3 + \ldots + \alpha_0 \alpha_1^l$$
$$A - \alpha_1 A = \alpha_0 - \alpha_0 \alpha_1^l$$

Hence, we have:

$$A = \frac{\alpha_0(1 - \alpha_1^l)}{1 - \alpha}.$$

Proceeding from here the infinite series denoted by B can be assessed:

$$B = \sum_{l=1}^{\infty} \frac{\dfrac{\alpha_0(1 - \alpha_1^l)}{1 - \alpha_1}}{R^l}$$

$$= \underbrace{\frac{\alpha_0}{(1-\alpha_1)R} + \frac{\alpha_0}{(1-\alpha_1)R^2} + \ldots}_{B_1} \underbrace{- \frac{\alpha_0\alpha_1}{(1-\alpha_1)R} - \frac{\alpha_0\alpha_1^2}{(1-\alpha_1)R^2} - \ldots}_{-B_2}$$

Again computing the sum of an infinite series we find:

$$B_1 = \frac{\alpha_0}{(1 - \alpha_1)(R - 1)} \text{ and } B_2 = \frac{\alpha_0\alpha_1}{(1 - \alpha_1)(R - \alpha_1)}$$

$$B = B_1 - B_2 = \frac{\alpha_0 R}{(R - 1)(R - \alpha_1)}$$

Finally, the last infinite series (denoted C) is:

$$C = \sum_{l=1}^{\infty} \left(\frac{\alpha_1}{R}\right)^l = \frac{\alpha_1}{R} + \left(\frac{\alpha_1}{R}\right)^2 + \left(\frac{\alpha_1}{R}\right)^3 + \ldots = \frac{\alpha_1}{R - \alpha_1}.$$

Thus, the rational expectations fundamental price of the stock is:

$$P_t^{rafu} = \frac{\alpha_0 R}{(R - 1)(R - \alpha_1)} + \frac{\alpha_1}{R - \alpha_1} Z_t.$$

PART II

Experiments and applications

6. Costly information and decision making

6.1 INTRODUCTION

Information costs were already an issue in the analysis of Chapter 4 where it was shown that only when information is sufficiently cheap does it become advantageous to use it and to rely on (informed) expectations. Here, we experimentally study a situation where this condition is met and find that many subjects fail to use information efficiently. This is particularly interesting since the set-up studied here gives ample room for learning. Among economists there is a strong notion that the opportunity to learn from experience will lead decision makers to fully rational behaviour. Conlisk (1996, p. 683) pointedly states this (not his) position as follows: 'Though people's rationality is bounded, they learn optima through practice, in the end acting as if unboundedly rational. Economists can take a shortcut to the outcome by assuming unbounded rationality from the start.' The experimental results documented here question this notion by documenting persistent efficiency losses when acquisition of information is costly. Repetition and learning is not sufficient to bring about rational choices.[1]

Decision making with costly information is related to the issue of decision costs. Radner (2000) uses the term 'costly rationality' to characterize decision making under uncertainty that optimally takes into account the costs of decision making. Pingle (1992, 2006) and Pingle and Day (1996) show that subjects resort to a variety of simplified problem-solving strategies if they bear costs of searching for a solution. The introduction of information costs in our experiment makes it possible to create a setting with a clearly defined optimal strategy. Hence, with information costs we can study (and test the optimality of) the path from ignorance to insight. In the experiment conducted here, subjects face a binary choice in a constant environment. This set-up eliminates complex feedback as a reason for suboptimal learning (see Timmermann, 1994). We also avoid another difficulty: Brehmer (1980) shows that there are important limits to learning when people face stochastic relationships.[2] He attributes the resulting misjudgements mostly to people's strong tendencies to search for deterministic rules.

We create a deterministic set-up favourable to this tendency. The problem studied here is similar to the categorization tasks psychologists have studied (see Barsalou, 1992).[3]

6.2   THE EXPERIMENTAL DESIGN

Subjects were given written instructions indicating the following (see Appendix 6.1 for the detailed instructions). Each subject starts with an initial wealth of 35 Swiss francs. The experiment runs for 24 periods. In each period the subject selects between two projects A and B. In any period one of these projects will be the winner while the other one will be the loser. If the winning project is chosen, the subject gains 2 francs and loses 2 francs in the opposite case. Which of the two projects is the winner depends potentially on three variables X, Y and Z.[4] In any period these variables take on either the value plus or minus. The plus and minus signs can stand, for example, for high and low levels of temperature or water level. While the causal structure of the situation remains constant throughout the experiment, this structure is initially unknown to the decision maker. In the instructions, subjects are guided through the different causal structures that potentially rule their (experimental) world. Here is a summary of these guidelines.

It is possible that the success of say A is conditional on one, two or all three variables having a specific sign. Consider as case I the situation where A is the winner only when all three variables have the plus sign (for example, X is +, Y is +, Z is +). Likewise (case II) it is possible that only two variables determine the success of A (for example, when X is + and Y is −). It can also happen (case III) that only one variable determines the success of A (for example, when X is +). Another possibility (case IV) is where among the three variables only one has to have a specific sign and in addition only one of the other two has to be of a specific sign (for example, when X is + and at least Y is − or Z is +). Yet another possibility (case V) is that any one of the three variables can guarantee the success of A if it is of the correct sign (for example, when at least one of the variables X, Y or Z is −). The five cases covered serve to indicate to the subject that it is manoeuvring in a world of necessary and sufficient causes. Cases I and II cover the situation where cues are necessary but not sufficient. Case III shows a situation where a condition is both necessary and sufficient. Case IV covers the situation where necessary but not sufficient cues are combined with cues that are neither necessary nor sufficient by themselves. In fact the case used in the experiment is from this class. Case V exemplifies the situation where variables are sufficient but not necessary causes. In a world as exemplified by these five cases, that is, ruled by (not) necessary and/or (not) sufficient cues and allowing for no exceptions to the rule, there are a total of 70 different causal structures given three possible cues. Appendix 6.2 shows all these causal structures (rules) and groups them according to the five cases given in the instructions.

Initially, subjects have no information on the values of the variables X, Y and Z. There is in fact no free information regarding X, Y and Z in the situation at hand. Instead, subjects have to decide which information they want to acquire and are charged a constant price per piece of information. The acquisition of information can be done sequentially. That is, it is possible to buy one piece of information and then to decide on further purchases of information. The cost of one piece of information is 0.25 francs. Hence, if a subject decides to acquire all information in a given period the associated costs are 0.75 francs. Information not acquired in a given period cannot be bought later (for example, temperature not measured on a given day cannot be measured the next day). Subjects were given an information sheet in which they could (if purchased) note the values of the cue variables as well as the outcomes in terms of the successful project. Subjects were also given two real-world scenarios that are represented by the stylized set-up of the experiment (for details see Appendix 6.1).

In the experimental setting the subject makes (and writes down) his or her choice after finishing the acquisition of information and is immediately informed on the correct choice, which is recorded in the column to the right of the explanatory variables (see Table 6.1). The experiment then proceeds to the next period. Table 6.1 shows the values of the variables X, Y and Z in all 24 periods. The reader can verify that the eight possible combinations of plus and minus are recycled in groups of eight but in changing order. Hence, the experiment shows every possible situation for a total of three times. The causal structure is clear after period seven: Y has to be + for project A to be successful and at least one of the other variables also has to have a positive sign.[5] The causal structural knowledge permits correct choices, provided information acquisition is continued, for periods 8 to 24.

Subjects had no cues regarding the likely frequencies of the various situations and they were under no time pressure during the experiment. With the logical structure chosen for the experiment the number of valid hypotheses (70 initially) regarding the structure is reduced as follows: 38 (period 1), 12 (period 2), 6 (period 3), 6 (period 4), 3 (period 5), 2 (period 6), 1 (period 7). Hence, given the information available in period 7 there is only one valid hypothesis left. Clearly, a different causal structure could lead to a different countdown in the elimination of hypotheses.

*Table 6.1   The information sheet filled with all available information and
the correct choices*

Periods	Variable X	Variable Y	Variable Z	The successful project	Your choice
1	+	−	+	B	
2	+	+	+	A	
3	−	+	−	B	
4	−	−	−	B	
5	+	+	−	A	
6	+	−	−	B	
7	−	+	+	A	
8	−	−	+	B	
9	−	+	−	B	
10	−	−	−	B	
11	−	−	+	B	
12	−	+	+	A	
13	+	−	+	B	
14	+	+	−	A	
15	+	−	−	B	
16	+	+	+	A	
17	+	−	+	B	
18	+	+	−	A	
19	−	+	+	A	
20	−	−	+	B	
21	−	+	−	B	
22	+	+	+	A	
23	−	−	−	B	
24	+	−	−	B	

6.3   OPTIMAL SOLUTION STRATEGY

Which strategy qualifies as the optimal strategy depends on the following
five parameters: (1) the difference in returns between the correct and the
incorrect choice; (2) the level of information costs; (3) the number of
periods in the experiment; (4) the sequence of combinations of XYZ shown
in the experiment; and (5) the causal structure relating X, Y and Z to A and
B. The parameter settings regarding (1), (2) and (3) used in the experiment
make starting the decision task with the acquisition of complete information (that is, the 'full information strategy') the right choice. Recall that the
instructions indicate clearly that there are only eight different possible combinations of plus and minus. Thus, one can be certain that situations

encountered will repeat after a maximum of eight periods and possibly earlier. Hence, information purchased will pay off sooner or later even if at the time information is purchased it may not facilitate the choice. With respect to parameter (4), the eight possible XYZ combinations are shown in the first eight periods so that building up a full understanding of the causal relationships is the result of full information purchase in the early part of the experiment. Clearly, alternative settings regarding parameters (1) to (4) could be chosen that would favour other strategies than the one leading to an understanding of the causal structure by way of information purchases.

The specific causal structure chosen for the experiment (that is, parameter 5) offers the possibility to identify redundant information as the experiment proceeds. Hence, optimal behaviour is characterized by a reduction of information costs through the switching from the 'full information strategy' to a 'lean information strategy'. The possible cost savings build on the fact that whenever Y is minus it is clear that B will be successful. Hence, in these cases one can make the correct judgement after spending just 0.25 francs on information. The subject has to buy additional information only in cases where Y is plus. A simple strategy for these cases is to buy the information on variable X (or Z) next. If this variable is also plus then one can safely stop information acquisition and opt for A.[6] If the second piece of information is a minus then information on the third variable has to be bought too. If this third variable is a plus, one knows that project A is the right choice, and if it is minus one has to opt for project B. Appendix 6.3 contains: (1) a proof for the claim that the full information strategy dominates choice without information under the given circumstances; and (2) details the cases of redundant information.

6.4   ANALYSIS OF INDIVIDUAL INFORMATION ACQUISITION

A total of 24 subjects participated in the experiment which was conducted in Switzerland. The first dozen participants consisted of non-economists (these subjects are denoted by P for 'people'). Among this group there were two business owners, two computer analysts, two commercial clerks, a bookseller, an architect, a nurse, a student of archeology, a linguistics graduate and a sales person. The second group consisted of graduate students in economics or recent PhDs in economics (these subjects are denoted by E) from the University of Bern. Before presenting the experimental results concerning choices with costly information it is important to note that in a dry run (see the instructions in Appendix 6.1) all subjects succeeded in making correct judgements when provided with full and free information. Hence, it is clear that all subjects involved in the experiment were able to use information (if freely offered) to make correct judgements.

Tables 6.2 and 6.3 display the data gathered in the experiment for the subjects of the two groups. The optimal course of information acquisition is presented on the left side of the two tables in three columns for X, Y and Z. The numbers in the columns refer to the ordering of purchases of items of information. Hence, in period 6 the numbers indicate that X should be purchased first, Z second and Y last. The instances where two different profiles of information acquisition are equally appropriate are those where there are two numbers in the same column. For example, for period 9 after acquiring Y it is equally appropriate to purchase X second and Z last or Z second and X last. If we contrast the described normative benchmark with the experimental data the following picture emerges:

1. Only a minority of subjects, namely three Ps and six Es, find (that is, learn) the optimal strategy of information purchase. Moreover, none of these subjects adopts the optimal strategy at the earliest opportunity (that is, in period 5). In the tables instances of optimal information choices are marked by a grey background. The best actual performance is shown by P9 who finds the optimal strategy as early as period 8. Three more subjects (all Es) follow closely, that is, in period 9.
2. An information-based, although non-optimal, strategy is followed by subjects E3 and E9 who summarize their insight into the determining structure by stating (in the post-experimental interview) that there need to be at least two adjoining cases of + for A to be the successful project. The heuristic followed by these subjects is less than optimal because they fail to infer that their (correct) observation implies that $Y = +$ is a necessary condition for the success of A. A similar strategy is followed by E10 who relies on the regularity that $X = -$ and $Z = -$ is a sufficient condition for B's success and hence, beginning in period 20, starts by purchasing X and Z.
3. Subjects E6 and E8 follow what can be called the 'main cue strategy'. They detect that Y is a necessary condition for A but make a misjudgement as to the financial implication of relying exclusively on this necessary but non-sufficient cue. Since in expected (and actual) terms there is a one in eight chance that Y as a cue is misleading, these subjects accept a loss of one-eighth times 4 francs per period (that is, 0.5 francs). In comparison to the optimal information strategy they save, on average, six or eight additional information charges of 0.25 francs each (that is, 0.1875 francs). Hence, they lose, on average, 0.3125 francs per period compared to the optimal strategy.

Table 6.2 Information acquisition by subjects of the group people

Period	OPTIMAL			P1			P2			P3			P4		
	X	Y	Z	X	Y	Z	X	Y	Z	X	Y	Z	X	Y	Z
1	1	1	1	1	1	1	1	1	1	1	1	1	2	2	1
2	1	1	1	1	1	1	1	1	1	1	1	1	1	2	1
3	1	1	1	1	1	1	1	1	1				1	1	1
4	1	1	1	1	1	1	1	1	1						
5	1	2	1	1	1	1	1	1	1				1	2	3
6	1	2	3	1	1	1	1	1	1					1	
7	1	3	2	1	1	1									1
8		1		1	1	1								1	
9	2 (3)	1	3 (2)	1	1	1				1	1	1		1	2
10	1	1	1	1	1	1								1	
11	1	1	1	1	1	1								1	
12	2	1	3 (2)	1	1	1									2
13				2	1										
14	2 (3)	1	(2)	2	1									1	
15					1									1	
16	2	1	(2)	2	1										
17					1										
18	2 (3)	1	(2)	2	1									1	
19	2	1	3 (2)	2	1	3								1	
20					1										
21	2 (3)	1	3 (2)	2	1	3									
22	2	1	(2)	2	1									1	2
23					1					1	1	1		1	
24	1	1			1										

Table 6.2 (continued)

Period	P5			P6			P7			P8			P9		
	X	Y	Z	X	Y	Z	X	Y	Z	X	Y	Z	X	Y	Z
1	1	1	1	1	1	1	1	1	1	1	1	1	1	1	1
2	2	1	2	1	3	2	1	1	1	1	1	1	1	2	3
3	1	3	2	1	1	1	1	1	1	1	1	1	1	1	1
4	2	1	1	1	1	1	1	1	1	1	1	1	1	1	3
5	3	1	2	2	1	1				1	1	1	1	2	3
6	2	1	3	1	1	1				1	1	1	1	2	3
7	1	2	1	2	2	1				1	1	1	1	1	
8	1	1	1	1	1	1				1	2	1	2	1	3
9	1	1	1	1	1	1				1	2	1	2	1	
10	1	1	1	1	2	2				1	2	1	2	1	3
11	1	1	1	1	1	1				1	2	1	2	1	
12	1	1	1	1	1	1				1	3	1	3	1	2
13	1	1	1	1	1	1				1	2	1	2	1	
14	1	1	1	1	1	1				2	2	1	2	1	
15	1	1	1	1	1	1				1	2	1	2	1	
16	1	1	1	1	1	1				1	2	1	2	1	3
17	1	1	1	1	1	1				2	3	1	2	1	
18	1	1	1	1	1	1				1	2	1	2	1	
19	1	1	1	1	1	1				2	1	1	2	1	3
20	1	1	1	1	1	1				1	1	1	2	1	
21	1	1	1	1	1	1				2	1	3	2	1	
22	1	1	1	1	1	1				3	1	2	2	1	
23	1	1	1	1	1	1				2	1		2	1	
24	1	1	1	1	1	1				1			1	1	

72

Period	P10			P11			P12		
	X	Y	Z	X	Y	Z	X	Y	Z
1	1	1	1	2	1	1	1	1	1
2	1	1	1		2	2	1	1	1
3	1	1	1		1		1	1	1
4	1	1	1	2		2	1	1	1
5	1	1	1	1	1		1	1	1
6	1	1	1			2	1	1	1
7	1	1	1		1	2	1	1	1
8	1	1	1		2		1	1	1
9	1	1	1	1	1	2	1	1	1
10	1	1	1		1	1	1	1	1
11	1	1	1		1	1	1	1	1
12	1	1	1		1	1	1	1	1
13	1	1	1		1		1	1	1
14	1	1	1		1	1	1	1	1
15	1	1	1	2	2	1	1	1	1
16	1	1	1	1	1	1	1	1	1
17	1	1	1		2		1	1	1
18	1	1	1		1	1	1	1	1
19	1	1	1	1	2	1	1	1	1
20	1	1	1		1	1	1	1	1
21	1	1	1		1		1	1	1
22	1	1	1		1	1	1	1	1
23	1	1	1		1	1	1	1	1
24	1	1	1		1	1	1	1	1

Table 6.3 Information acquisition by subjects of the group economists

Period	OPTIMAL			E1			E2			E3			E4		
	X	Y	Z	X	Y	Z	X	Y	Z	X	Y	Z	X	Y	Z
1	1	1	1	—	—	—	—	—	—	—	—	—	1	—	1
2	1	1	1	—	—	—	—	—	—	—	—	—	—	—	—
3	1	1	1	—	—	—	—	—	—	—	—	—	—	—	1
4	1	1	1	—	—	—	—	—	—	—	—	—	1	2	2
5	1	2	1	—	—	—	—	—	—	—	—	—	1	2	2
6	1	2	3	—	—	—	—	—	—	—	—	—	1	1	1
7	1	3	2	—	—	—	—	—	—	—	—	—	2	1	2
8	1	1	1	1	1	1	2	1	1	2	1	2	2	1	2
9	2 (3)	1	3 (2)	2	1	3	3	1	2	1	1	3	2	1	2
10															
11															
12	2	1	3 (2)	2	1	2	2	1	3	2	1	3	2	1	3
13															
14	2 (3)	1	(2)	2	1	1	2	1	1	1	1	1	2	1	2
15															
16	2	1	(2)	2	1	1	2	1	1	1	1	2	2	1	2
17															
18	2 (3)	1	(2)	3	1	2	2	1	3	1	1	2	2	1	3
19	2	1	3 (2)	2	1	2	2	1	1	1	1	1	2	1	1
20															
21	2 (3)	1	3 (2)	3	1	2	2	1	3	1	1	2	2	1	3
22	2	1	(2)	2	1	1	2	1	1	1	1	1	1	1	1
23															
24	1	1		1	1		1	1		1	1		1	1	

Period	E5			E6			E7			E8			E9		
	X	Y	Z	X	Y	Z	X	Y	Z	X	Y	Z	X	Y	Z
1	1	1	1	—	—	—	1	1	1	1	1	1	1	1	1
2	1	1	1	—	—	—	1	1	1	1	2	3	1	1	1
3	—	—	—	—	—	—	—	—	—	1	1	1	1	1	1
4	2	3	1	—	—	—	1	1	1	1	1	1	1	1	1
5	1	2	3	—	—	—	—	—	—	1	1	1	1	1	1
6	1	2	—	—	—	—	—	—	—	—	—	—	1	1	—
7	3	—	2	—	—	—	—	—	1	1	1	1	1	1	—
8	3	—	2	—	—	—	—	—	—	1	1	1	1	1	—
9	—	1	2	—	—	—	—	—	—	—	—	—	1	1	—
10	—	1	—	—	—	—	1	1	1	—	—	—	1	1	2
11	—	1	2	—	—	—	1	1	1	—	—	—	1	1	—
12	3	1	2	—	—	—	1	1	1	—	—	—	1	1	—
13	—	1	—	—	—	—	1	1	—	—	—	—	1	1	—
14	—	1	2	—	—	—	1	1	—	—	—	—	1	1	—
15	3	1	2	1	1	1	1	1	—	—	—	—	1	1	—
16	—	1	2				2	1	—				1	1	—
17	—	1	2				2	1	—				1	1	—
18	3	1	2				2	1	—				1	1	—
19	—	1	2				2	1	3				1	1	2
20	—	1	2				2	1	—				1	1	—
21	3	1	2				2	1	—				1	1	—
22	—	1	2				2	1	3				1	1	2
23													1	1	—
24							1	1	—				1	1	—

Table 6.3 *(continued)*

Period	E10			E11			E12		
	X	Y	Z	X	Y	Z	X	Y	Z
1	1	1		1	1	1	1	1	1
2	1	1		1	1	1	1	1	1
3	1	1		1	1	1	1	1	1
4	1		1	1	1	1	1	2	3
5	1	1	1	1	1	1	1	2	3
6	1			1	1	1	1	2	2
7	1	1	1	1	1	1	1	3	
8	1	1	1	1	1	1	1	1	1
9	1	1	1	1	1	1	3	1	2
10	1	1	1	1	1	1		1	
11	1	1	2	1	1	1		1	
12	1	1	1	1	1	1	2	1	3
13	1	1	1	1	1	1	2	1	
14	1	1	2	1	1	1		1	
15	1	1	2	1	1	1		1	
16	1	1	2	1	1	1	2	1	2
17	1	1	2	1	1	1		1	
18	1	1	1	1	1	1		1	
19	1	1	2	1	1	1		1	3
20	1	2	1	1	1	1	2	1	
21	1	1	1	1	1	1	2	1	
22	1	2	1	1	1	1		1	3
23	1	1	1	1	1	1	2	1	3
24	1	2	1	1	1	1		1	2

4. Five subjects (four Ps, one E) stick to the 'full information strategy' and lose 5 francs from period 9 to period 24 because they purchase redundant information.

5. Subjects P4 and P11 both suffer from the 'curse of missing knowledge'. They purchase information very selectively in the early part of the experiment and hence do not develop a full understanding of the causal relationships. Nevertheless, they benefit from the purchased information by inferring the special status of Y (subject P4) or by detecting that $Y=+$, $Z=+$ leads to A while $Y=-$ and $Z=-$ leads to B (subject P11).

6. The remaining subjects (P2, P3, P7) start the experiment with the full information strategy but give up information purchase before this investment bears results. P3 makes a (futile) attempt later in the experiment to gain insight by again purchasing all information.

6.5 ANALYSIS OF INDIVIDUAL PERFORMANCE

Table 6.4 shows the course of hits (indicated by 1) and misses (indicated by 0) of all 24 subjects. From periods 9 to 16 (periods 17 to 24) there are still nine (eight) subjects who mispredict the outcome at least once. These misses come from the subjects who either follow the 'main cue strategy', refrain from purchasing information, suffer from the 'curse of missing knowledge', or simply make mistakes like E10 who repeats the error of period 13 in period 17. The two lines at the bottom of the table show the total number of hits and the individual final pay-offs. While the number of hits ranges from a minimum of 10 to a maximum of 21, income ranges from 22.50 francs to 56.75 francs. The average income is 51.25 francs for the group of economists and 44.90 francs for the group of 'people'. The t-statistic for the hypothesis of equal means of incomes of the two groups is 2.03 which indicates that the two means differ significantly in a two-sided test when assessed at the 10 per cent critical level. When the test is based on income numbers for the last 16 periods only (that is, avoiding the element of hazard in the first eight periods) the value of the t-statistic rises to 2.20 which suggests a rejection of the hypothesis of equal means at the 5 per cent level of significance. The correlation between pay-off and time needed for the experiment is 0.006 and is not statistically different from zero.

The individual performances documented can be used to assess the average loss due to suboptimal decision making. In the terminology of Pingle and Day these are (information) misuse costs. For this purpose we calculate the gap between the optimal and actual return as a percentage of the optimal level. The calculations are based on the last 16 periods of the

Experiments and applications

Table 6.4 Successful choices and income by individual subject

Period	P1	P2	P3	P4	P5	P6	P7	P8	P9	P10	P11	P12
1	0	0	0	1	1	0	0	0	0	1	1	1
2	0	1	0	0	1	1	1	0	1	0	1	0
3	1	0	1	0	0	0	0	0	0	1	1	0
4	1	1	1	1	1	1	1	0	1	0	0	1
5	0	0	1	0	1	1	0	1	0	0	0	0
6	1	0	0	1	0	1	1	1	1	1	1	1
7	0	1	0	0	0	0	0	0	0	1	1	0
8	1	0	0	1	1	0	1	1	1	1	0	1
9	1	1	0	1	1	1	1	1	1	1	0	1
10	1	0	1	1	1	1	1	1	1	1	0	1
11	1	0	1	1	0	1	1	1	1	1	1	1
12	1	1	1	1	1	1	1	1	1	1	1	1
13	1	1	1	1	1	1	1	1	1	1	1	1
14	1	0	0	0	1	1	0	1	1	1	0	1
15	1	0	1	1	1	1	1	1	1	1	1	1
16	1	0	0	1	1	1	0	1	1	1	0	1
17	1	0	1	1	1	1	1	1	1	1	1	1
18	1	1	0	0	1	1	0	1	1	1	0	1
19	1	0	0	0	1	1	0	1	1	1	1	1
20	1	0	1	1	1	1	1	1	1	1	1	1
21	1	1	0	1	1	1	1	1	1	1	0	1
22	1	1	0	1	1	1	0	1	1	1	1	1
23	1	1	1	1	1	1	1	1	1	1	1	1
24	1	0	1	1	1	1	1	1	1	1	1	1
Total hits	20	10	12	17	20	20	15	19	20	21	15	20
Income	53	22	32	47	49	49	44	48	54	53	35	49
		1/2			1/2	1/2	3/4	1/2	3/4		1/4	

experiment because chance influences the average return over the first eight periods of the test. Specifically, since the eight possible *XYZ* combinations are shown a second time in the periods 9 to 16, and a third time in the periods 17 to 24, we compare the return over the second and the third showings with the normative benchmark. The return for eight periods (with all possible *XYZ* combinations) with the 'lean information strategy' is 12.5 francs (that is, eight times 2 francs as pay-off minus 14 times one-eighth of a franc as information costs). In comparison to this target income the loss suffered by members of the group of people is on average 44 per cent for the periods 9 to 16 and remains 40 per cent for the periods 17 to 24. The loss incurred by the group of economists is 20 per cent in the second third of the experiment and falls to 10 per cent in the last third. While economists, on

E1	E2	E3	E4	E5	E6	E7	E8	E9	E10	E11	E12
0	0	0	1	0	1	0	1	1	0	0	0
0	0	1	1	0	0	0	0	1	1	1	0
0	0	0	0	0	0	0	0	0	0	1	0
1	1	1	1	0	1	1	0	0	1	1	1
1	1	0	0	0	1	0	1	1	1	0	1
1	1	1	0	1	1	1	0	1	0	1	1
0	0	1	1	0	0	0	0	0	1	0	0
1	1	1	1	1	1	1	1	0	1	1	1
1	1	1	0	1	1	1	0	1	1	1	1
1	1	1	1	1	1	1	1	1	1	1	1
1	1	1	1	1	1	1	1	1	1	1	1
1	1	1	1	1	1	1	1	1	0	1	1
1	1	1	1	1	1	1	0	1	1	1	1
1	1	1	1	1	1	1	1	1	1	1	1
1	1	1	0	1	1	1	1	1	1	1	1
1	1	1	1	1	1	1	1	1	0	1	1
1	1	1	1	1	1	1	1	1	1	1	1
1	1	1	1	1	1	1	1	1	1	1	1
1	1	1	1	1	1	1	1	1	1	1	1
1	1	1	1	1	0	1	0	1	1	1	1
1	1	1	1	1	1	1	1	1	1	1	1
1	1	1	1	1	1	1	1	1	1	1	1
1	1	1	1	1	1	1	1	1	1	1	1
20	20	21	19	18	20	19	16	20	19	21	20
55	54	56	51	47	54	49	40	51	47	53	54
	3/4	3/4					3/4	3/4	3/4		1/2

average, learn to make better use of the resources, they continue to incur non-negligible losses. Both the size and the persistence of losses in the 'people' group are even more striking. Clearly, if one prefers to see the glass half full instead of half empty, one notes that 50 per cent of the non-economists and 75 per cent of the economists earned at least 90 per cent of the income from the optimal strategy.

6.6 CONCLUSIONS

Our results show that when individuals have to decide whether to become informed or not they often remain ignorant about the working of their environment. The experimental analysis shows that a majority of subjects fail to find the most economical way of forecasting the successful project among two possible prospects. This is particularly interesting since the experimental set-up consists of a simple deterministic relationship. The most important judgement error documented here is the incorrect assessment of the value of information, which in turn leads to an insufficient acquisition of information. Individuals who are subject to this type of error do not learn which action is most successful under any given condition. However, there are also cases of overacquisition of information. In this case individuals detect the causal structure of their environment but fail to implement this knowledge in the most efficient way. They invest in redundant knowledge.

In what kind of real-life situations is underacquisition of information likely to occur? Take education as an example: as in the experiment, the returns on educational investments mostly materialize in the future. In this situation some individuals (students) stop information acquisition after early experiences of not being able to use the pool of information already accumulated. The same problem may *mutatis mutandis* arise for producers and consumers. Learning about production techniques or qualities of goods takes time and often does not lead to immediate gains. Hence, the documented tendency for underinvestment in valuable and costly information is likely to impair many sorts of economic decisions. Overacquisition of information on the other hand is likely to be found, for example, among government officials or businessmen when it concurs, as in the experiment, with safe and significant pay-offs. Who bothers to attain maximum efficiency when things are going fine?

Considering instances of the two possible deviations from optimal behaviour, the case of underacquisition of information appears to matter more for economic performance. In many cases this tendency has significant and lasting detrimental effects on the accuracy of expectations and hence on the quality of judgements. The next chapter will explore how this suboptimality in decision making affects how cost–benefit analysis should be conducted. The provision of satellite information provides an interesting application for clarifying how welfare analysis should be conducted in the light of bounded rationality of agents.

NOTES

1. For contributions on incomplete learning see also, for example, Herrnstein and Prelec (1991), Cooper et al. (1997), Erev and Roth (1998) and Rabin (1998).
2. Brehmer's position has not remained unchallenged. More recent experiments suggest a much more optimistic view of people's ability to learn probabilistic relationships (see, for example, Shanks, 1995).

3. The set-up investigated here is not a market experiment. However, our results inform a debate between experiments on individual decisions and market experiments. It is well known from the literature (beginning with Allais, 1953) that individual behaviour in some situations is inconsistent with expected utility maximization. However, a large literature reports that market experiments are very often consistent with the market allocation implications of rational choice theory (for example, Plott, 1987). Experimental research (Cox and Grether, 1996) suggests that information feedback generated by markets and the repetitive nature of market tasks account for the positive results of market experiments. The experiment presented here involves feedback and repetition and thus satisfies the conditions prevailing in market experiments that are missing in most individual choice experiments. As it turns out, even with repetition there remains a significant fraction of agents who do not learn to behave rationally. Hence, the learning of the average player in a market is likely not the main reason when a market converges to the rational choice equilibrium. Rather, a correction of individual errors can occur in a market setting because some agents can take advantage of the errors of others.

4. The variables are identified by letters in order to prevent a transfer of notions concerning directions of causality from the real world.

5. Denote project A by 1, project B by 0, the plus sign as 1, and the minus sign as -1. The successful project can then be formally expressed as follows: successful project $= XY + YZ - XYZ$.

6. The experiment does not provide incentives for experimentation of the sort Mirman et al. (1993) have investigated; that is, there is no motive for a subject to risk a loss in order to learn about the structure of the situation.

APPENDIX 6.1   INSTRUCTIONS FOR THE EXPERIMENT (TRANSLATED FROM GERMAN)

In this experiment we study how individuals develop an understanding of the environment in which they have to make decisions. In our experiment a choice problem is studied. There are two possible projects (A and B) from which a choice has to be made in every period of the experiment. In each period exactly one of the two projects is successful. At the beginning of the experiment your starting capital is 35 francs. In each of the 24 periods of the experiment you can either earn 2 francs or lose 2 francs. If you choose what turns out to be the successful project you gain 2 francs and if you choose the other project you lose 2 francs. As a subject in the experiment you initially ignore which conditions lead to the success of A and B.

Which of the two projects is the successful one depends on the variables *X*, *Y* and *Z*. Each of these variables can, but does not have to, be an important factor for the success of A or B. The three variables can only take on the values + or −. It is possible that one, two, or even three of these variables have to take on a specific value for one of the projects to be the successful one. However, it is also possible that only two or just one of the three variables has to have a particular value to make one or the other project the successful one. As an example of the case where all three variables must be of a specific value, consider the case in which all variables have to be + in order to make A the successful project. The table shows for all possible combinations of *X*, *Y* and *Z* whether A or B is the successful project:

Variable *X*	Variable *Y*	Variable *Z*	The successful project
+	+	+	A
+	+	−	B
+	−	+	B
−	+	+	B
+	−	−	B
−	+	−	B
−	−	+	B
−	−	−	B

It is also possible that two variables determine the success of A and that the third variable is without any influence on the outcome. Consider as an example the case where *X* must be + and *Y* must be − for A to be successful. The next table shows for all possible combinations of *X*, *Y* and *Z* whether A or B is the successful project under the causal rules applicable here.

Variable X	Variable Y	Variable Z	The successful project
+	+	+	B
+	+	−	B
+	−	+	A
−	+	+	B
+	−	−	A
−	+	−	B
−	−	+	B
−	−	−	B

It is also possible that only one variable is decisive for the success of A and that the other variables do not matter for the success of A. Consider the example where X has to be + for A to be successful. Then the table of possible combinations looks as follows:

Variable X	Variable Y	Variable Z	The successful project
+	+	+	A
+	+	−	A
+	−	+	A
−	+	+	B
+	−	−	A
−	+	−	B
−	−	+	B
−	−	−	B

It is also possible that only one of the variables has to take on a specific value and that in addition only one of the remaining variables has to take on a particular value. We can, for example, have a world in which X must be + and in addition either Y must be − or Z must + to make A a success. Then the table of possible combinations looks as follows:

Variable X	Variable Y	Variable Z	The successful project
+	+	+	A
+	+	−	B
+	−	+	A
−	+	+	B
+	−	−	A
−	+	−	B
−	−	+	B
−	−	−	B

It is also possible that of the three variables each can be a sufficient condition for the success of a variable. As an example consider the case where of the three variables X, Y, Z at least one has to be – to make A the successful project. Then the table of possible combinations looks as follows:

Variable X	Variable Y	Variable Z	The successful project
+	+	+	B
+	+	–	A
+	–	+	A
–	+	+	A
+	–	–	A
–	+	–	A
–	–	+	A
–	–	–	A

Dry-Run Exercise

Here, you have the opportunity to work through an example to see whether you have understood the instructions. In the present exercise there are also two projects called L and M of which exactly one is the successful one in any period. In the table you see the values for three variables called T, U and V which can influence the success of L and M. In the present set-up

Period	Variable T	Variable U	Variable V	Your choice of project
1	+	+	+	
2	–	–	–	
3	+	–	+	
4	–	–	–	
5	+	–	–	
6	–	+	–	
7	–	–	+	
8	–	–	–	
9	–	+	–	
10	+	–	–	
11	–	–	+	
12	–	+	+	
13	+	–	+	
14	–	–	+	
15	+	+	+	

you know in advance that L is the successful project whenever U is − and V is +. In all other cases project M is successful. Hence, the variable T has no influence on the outcome. Please indicate for each of the 15 periods which of the two projects you judge to be the successful one.

(The responses to this exercise were compared to the correct classifications. Choices were correct in all periods for all subjects.)

The Experiment

This is where you decide for real, that is, for money. At the start you know nothing about the conditions for the success of the two available projects A and B. However, there is the opportunity to purchase information on the values of X, Y and Z in order to build up, if you so decide, an understanding of the conditions that lead A or B to success. Each piece of information, that is, knowledge whether for example X is + or − costs you a quarter of a franc. If you choose, for example, to inform yourself only on the value of X you give up 25 cents from your initial starting capital. If you choose to inform yourself on the values of all three variables you have to give up 75 cents. It is also possible to buy information sequentially: for example, you can spend 25 cents to learn the value of Z and afterwards (depending on the value of Z) decide whether you want to find out about X and afterwards possibly also purchase information on Y. The relationship between the variables X, Y and Z and the outcomes for A and B remains constant over the 24 periods of the experiment.

Consider two real-world scenarios that are represented by the set-up just described. One is the situation of an employee of a petroleum company who arrives in a foreign country and has to decide by noon every day (for 24 days) which of two production sites ought to be activated that day. Before noon the employee can acquire information regarding three variables which may help him to predict which of the operations A or B is the more successful that day. This information is gained by hiring and sending out local assistants. The other situation is the case of a Red Cross employee who arrives in a foreign country and has to decide every day whether to send the single available truck filled with medical supplies to hospital A or B given that at any day either hospital A or hospital B needs the supply more urgently.

You now have time to think about how you want to proceed. When you are ready, please indicate whether you want to buy information for period one. If you request information you can buy this information piecemeal. When you have all you need to make a decision you indicate what your choice is (and write it down in the last column of the information sheet provided below). Immediately afterwards you will be told whether A or B is the successful project in period one. You can write down this feedback in the 'successful project' column. Before the next choice there is sufficient time for reflection and the possible purchase of information.

Period	Variable X	Variable Y	Variable Z	The successful project	Your choice
1					
2					
3					
4					
5					
6					
7					
8					
9					
10					
11					
12					
13					
14					
15					
16					
17					
18					
19					
20					
21					
22					
23					
24					

APPENDIX 6.2   LIST OF CAUSAL RULES

Let A (B) be the successful project if the value of the function is 1 (0). These rules can be programmed with a software like Eviews. Rule C41 is the one used for the experiment.

genr C1 = 1*(X = 1)   genr C36 = 1*(X = 0 or Z = 1)
genr C2 = 1*(Y = 1)   genr C37 = 1*(Y = 1 or Z = 0)
genr C3 = 1*(Z = 1)   genr C38 = 1*(Y = 0 or Z = 1)
genr C4 = 1*(X = 0)   genr C39 = 1*(X = 1 or Y = 1)*(Z = 1)
genr C5 = 1*(Y = 0)   genr C40 = 1*(X = 1 or Y = 1)*(Z = 0)
genr C6 = 1*(Z = 0)   genr C41 = 1*(X = 1 or Z = 1)*(Y = 1)
genr C7 = 1*(X = 1 and Y = 1)   genr C42 = 1*(X = 1 or Z = 1)*(Y = 0)
genr C8 = 1*(X = 1 and Z = 1)   genr C43 = 1*(Y = 1 or Z = 1)*(X = 1)
genr C9 = 1*(Y = 1 and Z = 1)   genr C44 = 1*(Y = 1 or Z = 1)*(X = 0)
genr C10 = 1*(X = 0 and Y = 0)   genr C45 = 1*(X = 1 or Y = 0)*(Z = 0)
genr C11 = 1*(X = 0 and Z = 0)   genr C46 = 1*(X = 1 or Y = 0)*(Z = 1)
genr C12 = 1*(Y = 0 and Z = 0)   genr C47 = 1*(X = 0 or Y = 1)*(Z = 0)
genr C13 = 1*(X = 1 and Y = 0)   genr C48 = 1*(X = 0 or Y = 1)*(Z = 1)
genr C14 = 1*(X = 0 and Y = 1)   genr C49 = 1*(X = 0 or Z = 1)*(Y = 1)
genr C15 = 1*(X = 1 and Z = 0)   genr C50 = 1*(X = 1 or Z = 0)*(Y = 1)
genr C16 = 1*(X = 0 and Z = 1)   genr C51 = 1*(X = 0 or Z = 1)*(Y = 0)
genr C17 = 1*(Y = 1 and Z = 0)   genr C52 = 1*(X = 1 or Z = 0)*(Y = 0)
genr C18 = 1*(Y = 0 and Z = 1)   genr C53 = 1*(Y = 1 or Z = 0)*(X = 1)
genr C19 = 1*(X = 1 and Y = 1 and Z = 1) genr C54 = 1*(Y = 0 or Z = 1)*(X = 1)
genr C20 = 1*(X = 0 and Y = 0 and Z = 0) genr C55 = 1*(Y = 1 or Z = 0)*(X = 0)
genr C21 = 1*(X = 1 and Y = 0 and Z = 0) genr C56 = 1*(Y = 0 or Z = 1)*(X = 0)
genr C22 = 1*(X = 0 and Y = 1 and Z = 0) genr C57 = 1*(X = 0 or Z = 0)*(Y = 1)
genr C23 = 1*(X = 0 and Y = 0 and Z = 1) genr C58 = 1*(X = 0 or Z = 0)*(Y = 0)
genr C24 = 1*(X = 1 and Y = 1 and Z = 0) genr C59 = 1*(X = 0 or Y = 0)*(Z = 0)
genr C25 = 1*(X = 1 and Y = 0 and Z = 1) genr C60 = 1*(X = 0 or Y = 0)*(Z = 1)
genr C26 = 1*(X = 0 and Y = 1 and Z = 1) genr C61 = 1*(Y = 0 or Z = 0)*(X = 1)
genr C27 = 1*(X = 1 or Y = 1)   genr C62 = 1*(Y = 0 or Z = 0)*(X = 0)
genr C28 = 1*(X = 1 or Z = 1)   genr C63 = 1*(X = 1 or Y = 1 or Z = 1)
genr C29 = 1*(Y = 1 or Z = 1)   genr C64 = 1*(X = 0 or Y = 0 or Z = 0)
genr C30 = 1*(X = 0 or Y = 0)   genr C65 = 1*(X = 1 or Y = 0 or Z = 0)
genr C31 = 1*(X = 0 or Z = 0)   genr C66 = 1*(X = 0 or Y = 1 or Z = 0)
genr C32 = 1*(Y = 0 or Z = 0)   genr C67 = 1*(X = 0 or Y = 0 or Z = 1)
genr C33 = 1*(X = 1 or Y = 0)   genr C68 = 1*(X = 1 or Y = 1 or Z = 0)
genr C34 = 1*(X = 0 or Y = 1)   genr C69 = 1*(X = 1 or Y = 0 or Z = 1)
genr C35 = 1*(X = 1 or Z = 0)   genr C70 = 1*(X = 0 or Y = 1 or Z = 1)

Grouping of the causal rules according to the five examples given in the instructions:

Case I: All three cues have to have a specific value (that is, the case where all cues are necessary but not sufficient): C19, C20, C21, C22, C23, C24, C25, C26.

Case II: Two cues have to have a specific value and the third cue is without influence (that is, the case where some cues are necessary but not sufficient): C7, C8, C9, C10, C11, C12, C13, C14, C15, C16, C17, C18.

Case III: Only one cue has to have a specific value and the other cues are without influence (that is, the case where one condition is both necessary and sufficient): C1, C2, C3, C4, C5, C6.

Case IV: Only one cue has to have a specific value and in addition one of the other two cues has to have a specific value (that is, the case where necessary but not sufficient cues are combined with cues that are neither necessary nor sufficient by themselves): C39, C40, C41, C42, C43, C44, C45, C46, C47, C48, C49, C50, C51, C52, C53, C54, C55, C56, C57, C58, C59, C60, C61, C62.

Case V: Only one cue among several possible cues has to have a specific value (that is, the case where variables are sufficient but not necessary causes): C63, C64, C65, C66, C67, C68, C69, C70, C27, C28, C29, C30, C31, C32, C33, C34, C35, C36, C37, C38.

APPENDIX 6.3   PROOFS OF PROPOSITIONS

A6.3.1   Proof that Information Acquisition Stochastically Dominates Choice without Information

For the purpose of this proof the worst case for the strategy of information acquisition will be assumed: every possible situation (that is, combinations of X, Y and Z) is shown at least once and the causal structure is one in which knowledge of all three cues is necessary for correct judgement. (Note that nowhere do the instructions hint at it being more likely that only one (or two) rather than three cues could be important, let alone which of the three cues could be more important than the others. Hence, choices that are – in Bayesian terms – based on a skewed prior, given there is no reason to hold such a prior, cannot be considered rational.) It marks the worst case because it maximizes the number of times one has to guess. Consider, in contrast, the situation in which the same combination of X, Y and Z is shown 24 times. Under this scenario the strategy of information acquisition generates at least 23 correct choices. The worst case actually happens in the experiment and hence the experiment is in agreement with the assumption. In the case of guessing, the pay-off is the sum of 24 independent random variables with a mean of zero and a variance of 4. If, in contrast, one buys all the information then the pay-off is the sum of the first seven random variables (the same as with guessing) plus 17 certain pay-offs of 2 francs each, minus the amount 18 francs (24 times 0.75) for the purchase of all information. Thus we have traded the sum of 17 mean zero random variables for 16 francs. This argument does not take into account that the strategy of information acquisition might become cheaper (and hence gain) over time because of redundancy in information. This is the subject of the next subsection.

A6.3.2   Existence of Redundant Information and Implications for Information Acquisition

Definition: Information is redundant if a specific information unit (that is, a single entry for X, Y or Z) does not, given the combination of the other information units, affect the outcome.

The first time redundancy of information is revealed is in period 4 (see Table 6.1) when combination $- - -$ yields B given that in the previous period $- + -$ also yielded B. From this perspective it would be optimal for period 5 to start information purchase with X and Z hoping that both are $-$. If this were the case, purchase of Y could be saved for a correct choice. However, period 5 does not show the combination $X = -$, $Z = -$. Instead, period 5 presents another case of redundancy because the combination + + − results in A given that in period 2 + + + also leads to A. This implies that when $X = +$, $Y = +$, information regarding Z is redundant. Hence, for period 6 there is for the first time the possibility for an optimal sequential information purchase in three steps: given the described two cases of information redundancy it is advisable to purchase X first. As it is, it turns out + (suggesting the possibility of repetition of the case of period 2 or 5), which implies that the decision maker should then purchase Y in the hope that it is +. Since Y is − item Z also has to be purchased. No further form of redundancy is revealed in period 6 so that the optimal sequence of information acquisition in period 7 is the following. First purchase X. Given that it is negative, purchase Z next (hoping for a −). Since Z is + no error-free judgement can be made and hence Y has to be purchased too in order to realize a certain pay-off. After this the causal structure is clear and the optimal information acquisition is as described in the 'lean information strategy' (the case of period 8 is the last possible combination of cues and its outcome cannot be anything but B in a world with causal rules without exceptions).

7. Applied welfare economics with boundedly rational expectations

7.1 INTRODUCTION

This chapter draws out the implications for welfare analysis of the experimental findings of boundedly rational information acquisition reported in Chapter 6. Recent years have seen substantial and diverse contributions dealing with the analysis of forms, effects and models of bounded rationality in economics. Bounded rationality (as opposed to unbounded rationality) is the notion that at least some economic agents make suboptimal decisions because of their limited cognitive abilities. For a long time analysts have been mostly interested in how bounded rationality affects market functioning and policy effectiveness (see Conlisk, 1996; Selten, 1998, and Kahneman, 2003, for surveys). However, for some time after the early contributions by Simon (reprinted in 1983) relatively little has been written on the question of how bounded rationality influences the field of applied welfare economics. In recent years, however, this topic has gained importance. Closest to the application pursued here is the question of public provision of information addressed in Caplin and Leahy (2004). Another important application for findings regarding bounded rationality is the topic of savings policies (see Thaler, 1994; Laibson, 1997; Caplin and Leahy, 2003; Nyhus and Webley, 2006). Contributions like Rajeev and Fox (2002) and Jones (2003) document that not only economists but also researchers in the field of political science increasingly see the necessity of rethinking policy prescriptions in the light of bounded rationality. Our analysis here takes the issue of information acquisition to illustrate how findings of flawed decision making can be conceptually incorporated into welfare analysis.

The evidence documented in Chapter 6 shows that many individuals systematically underinvest in costly information that, considering the benefits of this information, should be purchased. More concretely, when subjects operate in a situation where they have to decide whether to purchase information or not many subjects: (1) decide to do without information altogether; or (2) quit the purchase of information after just a few periods because they become frustrated with the errors that are inevitable before a full understanding of the causal relationship between cues and outcomes is possible.[1] This tendency for underacquisition of costly information suggests that making information available freely has the potential to raise welfare. Underacquisition of information has also been documented and detailed by experimental research in psychology. Research on human decision making under uncertainty conducted by psychologists has revealed many cases where acquisition of information is individually and socially suboptimal. The cases of both underacquisition as well as overacquisition of information have been documented in the literature (see, for example, Connolly and Thorn, 1987; Newell et al., 2004). Much of this research has analysed so-called stopping rules that describe the behaviour of people who invest either more or less of their time before reaching a decision. Busemeyer and Rapoport (1988) show that it is cognitively particularly demanding for people to appreciate the value of extra information when they have to anticipate future decisions that are affected by this information. If this 'thinking ahead' is important to the given task, decision makers tend to stop the information search too soon.

The above-reported evidence is relevant when addressing the questions of who should provide information and how an information service could be financed. A welfare analysis proceeding on the assumption of perfect rationality would go astray and leave important issues in the provision of information services undetected. In contrast, the present welfare analysis takes the reported manifestation of bounded rationality (that is, underacquisition of costly information) into account and thereby identifies critical issues for producers, financiers and governments. We investigate whether a specific type of information should be provided as a public service or left to the private sector. The concrete type of information addressed here is so-called 'remote sensing information' which today is provided mostly through satellite information services.[2] This type of information is excludable in use. This feature gives rise to a situation where individuals have to decide whether they want to acquire this information and hence makes remote sensing information a potentially interesting application of the documented experimental findings. As we will see, the fact that this information can be non-rivalrous in use is what raises an important issue for welfare economics.

7.2   REMOTE SENSING

Remote sensing is the activity of measuring properties of an object from a distance. For more than 100 years the photographic camera was the most important device for remote sensing. From early on, the view from afar and from above was possible from balloons. Soon planes took over as means of positioning cameras so as to gather interesting information. From the very beginning many of the technologies in the field of remote sensing were developed with military applications in mind and with military funding.[3] In 1960 the first non-photo sensor was launched as a meteorological satellite. In 1972 the first in a series of satellites (later named LANDSAT) was launched and since then other satellite-based sensors, notably the French Système Probatoire d'Observation de la Terre (SPOT), have been placed in orbit. So far, the larger part of research and investments in satellite information systems has taken place in the US, and the National Aeronautics and Space Administration (NASA) has played a decisive role as an institutional coordinator and sponsor of activities.[4] In the US of the early 1980s the increasing importance and costs of satellites initiated discussions on the public-good character of remote sensing data. This topic was raised by the US Congress (see Office of Technology Assessment, 1984) and as a conclusion of this analysis legislation known as the Land Remote Sensing Commercialization Act of 1984 started an era with an increased role of the private sector. As a result, the prices of LANDSAT information rose and significantly reduced the information demand by private users (see Gabrynowicz, 2003). The last 20 years have seen a series of legal changes that have returned LANDSAT back to the public sector. One reason for what many see as a failed and improper commercialization of space data was the notion behind the 1984 legislation that information that is non-rivalrous in consumption but excludable should be privately offered and priced. As described in the previous section, this sort of information is liable to be underproduced because of bounded rationality of users in a purely commercial setting. For the specific analysis of public policies toward private underinvestment in satellite information we turn to agriculture, a particularly relevant field where (excludable) remote sensing data is used.

Farming has been an early application of remote sensing and is seen by many experts as one of the most promising topics of application for the future.[5] Information on many aspects of crop health (for example, plant stress related to moisture, nutrients and diseases) can be gathered by satellites because objects reflect electromagnetic waves which makes it possible to identify their nature and quality. Clearly, the connection between electromagnetic information and surface quality is a matter of very sophisticated biophysical research.[6] Current technology permits satellites to provide information on surface quality with a one-metre resolution or better. Remotely sensed information is typically combined with information from the global positioning system (GPS) and with a computer-equipped tractor on the ground. Besides this very advanced use of information there certainly also exist simpler ways to use satellite information in agriculture. At present, remote sensing in agriculture is widely discussed but not widely adopted. The following analysis explores bounded rationality as one impediment to the adoption of this new technology and explores possible policy responses.

7.3   COST–BENEFIT ANALYSIS OF THE PROVISION OF REMOTELY SENSED DATA

Assume that information with a high degree of precision on crop health can be gathered either on the ground or by remote sensing. That is, either the farmer goes out and measures crop health on the ground or the same crop features are remotely sensed and electronically transmitted to the farmer. Let us look at a situation with n producers with identical farms. Assume further that having precise information on crop health raises the farmer's discounted stream of income (that is, his wealth) by p (measured for example in dollars) because he can take measures (watering, fertilizer, pesticides) to increase his harvest.[7] However, the cost of private or individual information gathering is c (where $c > p$). Hence, the strategy of individual acquisition of high-precision information is never pursued and farmers base their decisions on more general information only. If, in contrast, a collective of n producers sets up a service for remotely sensed data they incur a substantial fixed cost C but – as an approximation – bear zero cost for informing an extra producer and also zero cost for maintaining the service.[8] Hence, the aggregate cost curve for the centrally provided data in Figure 7.1 is flat: costs do not increase with a larger collective of producers. If all farmers use the remote sensing information, the sum of extra discounted revenue rises with an increase in the number of producers at a rate of p. Figure 7.1 shows the total benefit of the information service as a function of the size of the collective of producers. Let us turn to the question of how rational producers behave in this environment. They will voice their willingness to participate in a collective scheme on the premise that the costs are shared fairly and the cost of participation is less than the benefit p. Hence, if producers are rational the cost–benefit analysis is simple: we can determine a critical (minimal) size for the collective $n^* = C/p$ to make the central provision of information optimal. For collectives smaller than n^* doing without high-precision information (that is, a decision against acquisition of precision data) is optimal. For a collective of farmers with $n < n^*$ the size of the group of users is simply too small to justify the large set-up cost. If the service is adopted it is financed by a fee of size C/n that diminishes with the size of the collective.

Now let us turn to the experimentally documented relevant form of bounded rationality, that is, of information underacquisition. For the present

a) With full rationality

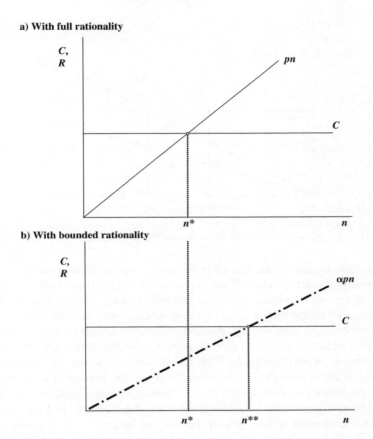

Figure 7.1   Cost–benefit analysis

purpose, it is easiest to think of a fraction α of farmers who are able – before actually having experienced it – to assess correctly the value of the precision information.[9] Hence, for any number n of producers there is only a number αn who are willing to participate in the remote sensing data service. The other producers, $(1 - \alpha)n$ in number, will show no willingness to pay for the service of remotely sensed data. They simply (and wrongly) see no value in this infor- mation. If asked they will vote against participation in such a collective scheme. Since access to the remotely sensed information can easily be made dependent on participation (that is, there exists the technological possibility to exclude non-payers) there is no incentive on the part of producers to under- state their interest in the collective information service. Hence, with a non- zero fraction of boundedly rational producers the curve of the aggregate

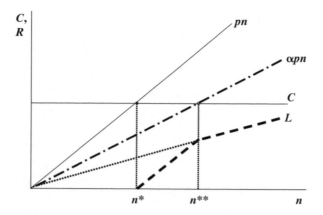

Figure 7.2   Social loss due to bounded rationality

willingness to pay for the service in Figure 7.1 will be flatter than under full rationality. In fact the slope of the curve – shown in the lower panel of Figure 7.1 – is αp compared to p under full rationality. As a result, it takes a larger collective of farmers $n^{**} = C/\alpha p$ for the centralized service to be adopted. For collectives larger than n^{**}, the number of rational agents is large enough so that the service is set up. Still, even with a collective larger than n^{**} there is a loss of potential income. This loss is due to the output foregone by those not smart enough to participate in the service. For the rational players this inefficiency takes the form of excessively high membership fees. Quantitatively, for collectives of a size $n > n^{**}$ the aggregate loss is $L = n(1 - \alpha)p$. Collectives of a size ranging between n^* and n^{**} will not adopt the service with a resulting loss (in terms of discounted unearned net income) of $(n - n^*)p$. Figure 7.2 shows the social loss as a broken line. Here it shows that the potential benefit of some form of intervention (to be discussed) raises monotonically with the size of the group of producers.

7.4   HOW CAN WELFARE LOSSES BE AVOIDED?

Here we study schemes that help to prevent the loss of income due to boundedly rational producers. We first look at a possible solution that can emerge from within the private sector: with $n > n^*$ smart producers can in principle set up the service and offer its use to their boundedly rational colleagues for a trial period free of charge. After this trial period the reluctant producers will have experienced the benefit of the service and will be prepared to share in its cost. Thus, the social loss vanishes and the output gain

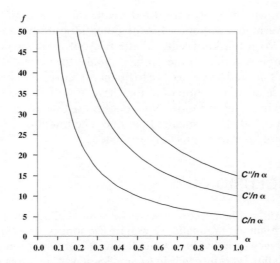

Figure 7.3   Necessary financial resources as a function of the fraction of rational producers

can be divided over all (new and old) participants.[10] However, this scheme only functions if smart producers have enough funds to set up the service on their own. If their personal liquid wealth is insufficient, a financier (banker) will need to step in. Hence, banks become an important partner in setting up the information service. If banks – and the capital market – are able to provide the necessary funds, the information service will be set up and welfare losses are avoided. If, however, the capital needs of the project initiators (that is, the rational producers) cannot be satisfied (because, for example, of a lack of collateral) there will be a need for government intervention. This can take the form of lending by a specialized institution, like the World Bank or another development bank.[11]

Consider the display of Figure 7.3 to appreciate the interplay of bounds to rationality and bounds to producers' financial resources: here, the fraction of rational producers is plotted along the horizontal axis. Along the vertical axis we plot the financial resources per producer ($f = C/n\alpha$) that need to be obtainable. Clearly, the smaller the fraction of rational producers, the larger is the level of necessary financial resources they have to raise. Higher levels of C (C' and C'', respectively, indicate a doubling and a tripling of set-up costs) visualized in two isoquants farther to the northeast clearly sharpen the problem of financing the information service at any level of α. If the average rational producer cannot raise financial resources (saved and borrowed) of at least f we have a situation where a private sector solution (even with possibly subsidized credit) will lead to welfare losses.[12] How can government prevent a loss of potential output under these circumstances? With full knowledge of the relevant parameters C, p and n there is a simple solution to the problem: make the service obligatory in cases where $n > n^*$ and levy a tax C/n to finance it. Given that producers will make good use of information once they have it, welfare will be improved by this government intervention. Note once more that all that needs to be known about α is that it is smaller than one. The fraction of rational producers does not need to be precisely estimated.

7.5   CONCLUSIONS

The analysis offered here indicates ways to relate findings of specific manifestations of bounded rationality to welfare economics. The experimentally reported tendency of individuals to underinvest in information in situations where information is costly can lead to significant welfare losses. Social planners who maintain the assumption of full rationality of agents in such cases will fail to identify potentially important issues for public policy. This chapter provides an alternative analysis that explicitly takes into account bounded rationality of producers. Based on this perspective the provision of satellite data in agriculture is identified as an exemplary field for three reasons: (1) remote sensing information is widely predicted to play a growing role in agricultural development; (2) providing such high-resolution information necessitates large investments; and (3) bounded rationality of producers is likely to interact with bounded access to financial resources, particularly in developing countries. As a general finding from this analysis we conclude that exploring and accounting for the bounded rationality of information users can be a key element in the design of public policies that successfully blend public funding with private initiative and commercial interests.

NOTES

1.   Some subjects in the experiment indeed overinvested in information. However, the magnitude of this inefficiency is very small in comparison to the cases of underinvestment. Agents who consistently purchase information in such a forward-looking task are able economizers who, if at all, buy only small amounts of irrelevant information and even then often learn to avoid this wasteful behaviour.
2.   So far the economics profession has given very limited attention to the subject of provision of satellite information (see Macauley and Toman, 1991, for an exception).
3.   See Hays (2002) for a more general perspective on space-based military assets.
4.   Satellite information is of increasing importance in many important areas like transportation planning (Usher and Truax, 2001), the tracking of erosion processes (Hill and

Schütt, 2000), deforestation (Saatchi et al., 1997) and related fire risk assessment (Sannier et al., 2002) to name just a few applications.

5. The field of 'precision farming' or 'precision agriculture' encompasses many different new technologies in addition to remotely sensed data. See Ludowicy et al. (2002) and the National Research Council (1997) for surveys.

6. The two periodicals *Journal of Remote Sensing* and *Remote Sensing of Environment* publish much of the research in the field.

7. Given this set-up with clearly quantified and identical individual benefits of the information service we do not have to deal with the issue that potential users of publicly provided remote sensing data have an incentive to understate their benefit from the service in order to free-ride on others.

8. The set-up cost C includes costs for satellite technology and satellite launching. Typically a commercial satellite will offer information for several collectives of producers (with different information needs) and several satellites will be involved in any single service.

9. In the experiment of Chapter 6 α is 0.6 for the group of non-economists and 1 for the group of economists. Clearly, the size of α is an empirical matter. For the present study α does not have to be estimated but the analysis gains its relevance from the assumption that α is below 1. A reading of surveys of the field of precision agriculture makes clear that the teaching of the new technological opportunities to farmers is a major challenge. Thus, as a practical matter it should be understood that the process of gaining insight in the advantages of this new form of information takes time. Hence, a full use of the new methods will necessitate substantial and continuing training and educational investments (see National Research Council, 1997). For the initial step toward adoption that is the subject of the present analysis, '(i)t will be very important for systems and data products to be based on crop producer needs and for provision to be made for farmers and others to develop an understanding of remote sensing' (National Research Council, 1997, p. 38).

10. For this welfare analysis it is not necessary (nor probably very realistic) to assume that the same conditions apply to latecomers as to the initiators of the service. Discriminating latecomers by asking for a transfer of some their production gains does not make such a scheme inefficient.

11. See Byamugisha and Zakout (2000) for a discussion of related issues.

12. It has to be kept in mind that the cost of applying remote sensing information does not only consist of paying for the information service. Financial resources of producers are also strained by substantial investments for additional technology on the ground.

8. Pattern recognition as the basis of expectations

8.1 INTRODUCTION

Here we investigate the role visual patterns play when people face the task of assessing the course of future events. The recognition of patterns and the reliance on patterns has been documented to be important in many aspects of human behaviour. Psychology offers a detailed analysis of the many uses of patterns (that is, shapes, forms) in classification tasks as well as the cognitive and neural architecture supporting it (see, for example, Puccetti, 1974; Rumelhart et al., 1986; Posner, 1989; Lund, 2001). Humans detect patterns quickly, and systematically base their decisions on inferences drawn from patterns. Clearly, the ability to recognize similarities in observations (occurrences), and the capacity to take appropriate action rapidly, has high survival value for any organism. In the economics profession Herbert Simon was the first to see clearly the importance of pattern recognition for the understanding of decision making (see Simon, 1959, 1983, and also Frantz, 2003). While Simon considered recognition of complicated patterns important for the decision making of experts, experiments conducted by psychologists have documented that simple patterns play an important role in time series forecasting of non-experts (see, for example, Feldman, 1963; Jones, 1971, and Eggleton, 1982).

The analysis presented here explores the notion that humans rely on pattern recognition when it comes to forecasting (or foreseeing) economic events. Specifically, we explore the idea that humans regularly extrapolate based on simple patterns they observe in time series instead of searching for structural relationships in the data. This type of forecasting behaviour should be distinguished from the time-consuming 'technical analysis' that professional chartists apply (see, for example, Lo et al., 2000). The present chapter can thus be seen as analysing the behaviour of 'natural born chartists'. We develop a specific model of pattern use and estimate parameters using individual data. This model makes it possible to identify various expectation styles. Data for the purpose of estimation are gathered in an experiment in which both a clearly defined substantively rational solution and the possibility to use patterns exist. We also consider how the experimental data can be related to issues of financial markets, a topic that will be further developed in Chapter 9. The model of pattern-based expectations formation proposed here is a new variant in the list of extrapolative expectations schemes discussed in Chapter 5.

8.2   A MODEL OF PATTERN USE

Pattern-based prediction has three aspects: (1) what constitutes a pattern; (2) what types of patterns are used in intuitive forecasting; (3) how expectations are affected by specific patterns. The simplest set-up for clarifying these issues is a binary series x whose elements take on only the values zero and one. Here, a pattern in a general sense is any specific sequence of zeros and ones of length n. Hence, at any point in time the preceding n observations make up one particular pattern. Note that this general definition of what constitutes a pattern does not single out types of patterns that are regularly being relied on in actual forecasting. The prominence of some types of patterns from a behavioural viewpoint will be addressed in sections 8.4 and 8.5. An example for a pattern of order two is $x_{t-1} = 0$ and $x_t = 1$ denoted as 01. Imagine a situation where a person has to predict the outcome of the series x. Specifically, given a past sequence of zeros and ones, at time t person j is asked to give probability $P_j(x_{t+1} = 1)$ denoted by $P^1_{j,t+1}$. An uninformed (or unreflected) response to this problem is a probability assessment of 0.5. The first part of the hypothesis of pattern-based expectations is that a given person is a pattern associator of order n. The simplest way to use a pattern is the following: whenever the series produces a sequence of zeros and ones which forms a pattern that the decision maker judges as reliable for forecasting, he infers that in the next period the value one occurs with a constant pattern-specific probability different from 0.5. This is called a 'fixed pattern response'. It involves no learning.[1] The individual approaches the prediction task with a certain view (or approach) and does not change it. In order to formally describe such behaviour we define the dummy variables:

$$D^{n,i}_t = \begin{cases} 1 \text{ if } x_t, \ldots x_{t-n+1} \text{ form pattern } i \\ 0 \text{ otherwise} \end{cases}. \tag{8.1}$$

So, for any point in time t the indexed dummy variables tell which pattern appears at that point in time. Our model of fixed pattern response can be stated as:

$$P^1_{j,t+1} = 0.5 + \sum_{i=1}^{m} \alpha^i_j D^{n,i}_t. \tag{8.2}$$

Here, $P^1_{j,t+1}$ denotes the subjective probability of the value one reported by individual j at time t for time $t+1$. The parameter m denotes the number of different patterns on which the individual relies. The parameters α^i_j measure to what extent the subject's probability assessment deviates from 0.5 at the occurrence of pattern i.

8.3   THE EXPERIMENT

In the experiment subjects are shown a time series that consists of only ones and zeros. Subjects are instructed to assess the probability of the two possible values for the subsequent period.[2] It is pointed out to them (in written instructions and reiterated orally) that the task is not to guess the outcome of the next period but to provide, at every step of the experiment, the best possible estimates of the two probabilities (that is, to express the reasoned confidence in the two possible outcomes). The financial compensation of subjects depends on the accuracy of their probability estimates. A Markov chain with constant transition probabilities was used to generate the data in the experiment. Appendix 8.1 contains the instructions given to participants in the study.[3] The transition probabilities (unknown to the subjects) of the Markov chain used in the experiment are depicted in Table 8.1.

A section headed by 'extra information' pointed to the data-generating process. This extra information stated that 'the following is known about the process that has produced the data in this experiment: the probabilities that the values one or zero will be realized in the next period depend only on the value the series has in the current period'. Furthermore, subjects were given the first three observations of the process. Subjects were asked to start (after 15 minutes of reflection) the experiment by giving their probability assessment for period 4. Thereafter, they were provided with the outcome for period 4 and had 60 seconds to decide on the probabilities for period 5, and so on up to period 50. The display of the series which was used in the experiment is shown in Figure 8.1. The upper panel shows the series as the subject observes it at the beginning of the experiment and

Table 8.1   Transition probabilities of the Markov chain

from \ to	0	1
0	0.35	0.65
1	0.55	0.45

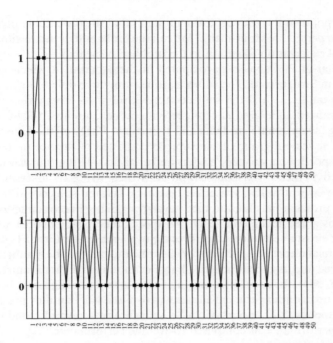

Figure 8.1   The series as seen at the beginning (above) and after the last period (below) of the experiment

the lower panel shows the course of x over the full course of the experiment.

In order to solve the problem optimally, subjects first had to infer from the 'extra information' that the data-generating process was a Markov chain. This information clearly excludes a Bernoulli process (an alternative process with fixed parameters) by stating that the likely outcome of the series depends on the preceding value of the series. In this situation the substantively rational solution consists of estimating the parameters of the data-generating process by the method of maximum likelihood.[4] This parameter estimation is very simple: subjects need to keep a record of the frequency with which the four possible moves (from one to one, from one to zero, from zero to one, and from zero to zero) of the series occurred. The probabilities for the next period can be calculated based on the relative frequencies and the value of the series in the current period. As an example, consider the case of period 14: the series up to period 14 is 01111101010100. Up to this point in time the series has moved from one to one four times, from one to zero four times, from zero to one four times, and from zero to a zero only a single time. Since the series is on the value zero at point 14 the relevant estimate states that the probability of a one to occur in period 15 is four-fifths.[5] We call the probabilities thus estimated the rational expectations solution to the problem presented.

A total of 30 subjects participated in the experiment which was conducted in Switzerland. The subjects came from three different professional backgrounds: the first ten subjects were economists. This group included one advanced undergraduate, one recent graduate not involved in graduate training, six graduate students and two recent PhDs of the University of Bern. The second group of ten subjects consisted of finance professionals (that is, portfolio managers, traders and analysts). This group was included on the hypothesis that people who earn their living by assessing trends should perform well at the given task. The last ten subjects were neither finance professionals nor did they have any training in economics or statistics. This group included a teacher, a speech therapist, a dentist, an architect, a dentist's secretary, a hairdresser, two secretaries, a roof-layer and a commercial clerk. For purposes of identification in the study subjects were numbered and assigned the letter E (for economists), F (for finance professionals), or P (for people) according to the group to which they belonged. At the end of the experiment subjects were asked whether they preferred an instantaneous cash reward of 25 Swiss francs or a reward based on individual performance as compared to average performance.[6]

8.4   EVALUATING THE RESPONSES

We start by addressing the issue of substantive rationality. In the present experiment no subject ventured into estimating a Markov process. This became clear in two ways: during the experiment none of the subjects kept a record of the frequencies with which the four possible moves of the series occurred. In addition, in the post-experimental interview all subjects indicated that they had not tried to estimate transition probabilities of a Markov process. The 'as if' argument that the substantively rational solution could provide a reasonable approximation was rejected by comparing the sum of squared deviations of the subjects' responses from the rational expectations solution to the sum of squared deviations from a constant value of 0.5. For 28 out of 30 subjects the squared deviations from the value 0.5 were, on average, smaller than the squared deviations from the rational expectations values.[7] This indicates that, in the present set-up, suboptimal use of information is the rule rather than the exception. This result contradicts the conclusions drawn by Dwyer et al. (1993) who interpret their experimental findings as largely consistent with rational expectations. The present study is clearer than that, for example, by Dwyer et al. at stating all available information to the subjects. Moreover, the optimal use of information is simple and subjects lack no technical tool with which they could easily improve their forecasts (that is, estimation of transition probabilities does not necessitate the use of a computer). Thus, the present findings add evidence against the hypothesis of rational expectations.

Next, we turn to a description of the various heuristical procedures used by subjects. For this purpose subjects answered several questions after the experiment. Subjects were asked whether they could give an algorithm that would describe their responses. Six subjects answered this question affirmatively and supplied their algorithms which were all – like, for example, the estimation of the probabilities of a Bernoulli process – based on erroneous reasoning. Since we have the algorithms generating the responses of these six subjects, no statistical models are estimated for these participants in the next section. The remaining 24 subjects who were not able to give a simple description of their behaviour were then asked how they had reached their answers period by period. All these subjects reported using visual patterns. The most frequently reported (by 21 subjects) patterns were runs of ones or zeros. Additionally, 15 subjects reported using zigzag patterns, that is, patterns of repeated instantaneous change. That runs and zigzags are the most prominent of all visual patterns has been repeatedly documented in the literature (see Feldman, 1963; Jones, 1971, and Eggleton, 1982). Six subjects reported relying on long waves which consist of a run of one number followed by a run of the other number, and four subjects relied on short waves, that is, sequences like 001100 or 011011. In addition, 21 subjects reported that they typically gave equal probabilities (that is, fifty-fifty) to the two possible outcomes when the series seemed unpredictable. Several subjects adopted this cautious stance when others relied on zigzag patterns. Especially, many of the finance professionals stated that they recognized zigzag patterns but did not use them – and instead behaved cautiously – because they thought of it as a period of market perturbations.

8.5   ESTIMATES OF INDIVIDUAL PATTERN USE

In this section we investigate the experimental data econometrically in order to analyse whether the reliance on patterns reported in the previous section can – at least in part – be captured by the model of fixed pattern response of equation (8.2). The specification of the individual models is the result of a statistical search procedure. The first step in the sequential search consists of determining the adequate n for a subject. This is done by estimating equation (8.2) for every subject for levels of n from 2 to 5. A higher number of n would mean that several of the possible patterns would not show up in the experimental series.[8] Moreover, there is a potential problem with degrees of freedom in the estimation: the total number of all possible patterns (in the general sense defined in section 8.2) for a given n is 2^n. This implies that for $n = 5$ (the largest n considered here) there would be a total of 32 parameters to be estimated if all possible patterns were considered. This would not be feasible given the experimental data at hand. In this situation the number of patterns included in the regressions is limited to a subset of possible patterns that are relevant for behaviour. Here, we rely on earlier psychological research (for example, Feldman, 1963; Jones, 1971, and Eggleton, 1982) and on the post-experiment interview to limit the number of patterns considered: the most prominent patterns are runs and zigzag patterns. This means that we set the parameter $m = 4$ for all subjects instead of estimating it statistically. The patterns considered then for $n = 2$ are 11, 01, 00, 10, for $n = 3$ the corresponding patterns are 111, 101, 000, 010, for $n = 4$ the patterns are 1111, 0101, 0000, 1010, while for $n = 5$ the patterns are 1111, 10101, 0000, 01010. Note that the patterns ending on a one (like 01 and 11) mean that the value of the series observed by the subject at time t is a one (that is, $x_t = 1$) while patterns ending on zero (like 00 and 10) imply that $x_t = 0$. Appendix 8.2 lists, as an example, the values of $D_t^{3,i}$ used in the statistical analysis.

Regression models were estimated for the 24 subjects who could not give a mathematical expression describing their responses. Table 8.2 reports the resulting individual models. It turns out that nine subjects use $n = 2$, seven subjects use $n = 3$, five subjects rely on patterns of length $n = 4$ and two subjects rely on patterns of length $n = 5$. Hence, the majority of subjects base forecasts on relatively short patterns. It is further worth highlighting that the expectation of a continuation of a run is more prevalent than the expectation of a breakdown of a run. This is witnessed by the number of positive (negative) parameter values measuring the responses to runs of ones (zeros). Among those 17 subjects whose estimated coefficients for the individual are jointly statistically significant 11 (ten) subjects expect a one (zero) to show up after a run of ones (zeros) while only five (seven) subjects expect a zero (one). Judged by the three groups of subjects the group 'people' is the only group for which the above statement should be replaced by the statement that equal numbers expect a pattern break as expect a pattern continuation. Similarly, a majority of subjects expect a zigzag pattern like 1010 to continue (here, for example, to be likely followed by a one). Furthermore, for a majority of subjects pattern responses are found to be qualitatively and quantitatively symmetric: this means that when in response to a pattern like 111 subjects foresee a one to occur with probability β, they foresee the same outcome (a one) after pattern 000 with probability $0.5 + (0.5 - \beta)$. Likewise if they foresee a one to occur with probability γ after pattern 101, they foresee a one to occur after pattern 010 with probability $0.5 + (0.5 - \gamma)$. This

Table 8.2   Estimates of individual models of pattern responses

Pattern Subject	11/111/1111/ 11111	01/101/0101/ 10101	0/00/000/0000/ 00000	10/010/1010/ 01010	n	R^2
E3*	0.153	−0.150	0.250	0.150	4	0.153
E4	0.005	−0.176	−0.083	0.169	4	0.185
E5*	0	−0.250	−0.500	0.500	3	0.235
E6*	−0.300	−0.187	0.375	0.291	5	0.276
E9*	0.277	−0.020	−0.300	−0.020	4	0.300
E10*	0.021	0.081	−0.333	−0.109	2	0.227
F2*	−0.292	−0.083	0.183	−0.044	3	0.548
F3*	0.147	0.072	0.166	0.027	3	0.113
F4*	0.130	0	−0.266	0.016	3	0.524
F5	−0.350	0	0.500	0.166	5	0.148
F6	0.047	0.054	−0.016	0.018	2	0.012
F7*	0.171	0.068	−0.291	−0.159	2	0.428
F8*	0.199	−0.075	−0.250	0.113	2	0.246
F10*	0.227	−0.093	−0.138	−0.027	2	0.372
P1	−0.400	0	0.500	0.166	5	0.086
P2*	−0.307	0	−0.500	0.333	3	0.232
P3	−0.277	0.300	0.500	−0.100	4	0.145
P4	0	−0.150	0.125	0.150	4	0.092
P5*	−0.268	−0.062	0.166	0.458	3	0.231
P6*	−0.444	−0.357	−0.166	−0.375	2	0.304
P7*	0.311	−0.079	−0.311	0.217	3	0.428
P8*	0.394	0.409	0.375	−0.045	2	0.407
P9*	0.225	0.175	0.222	0.040	2	0.070
P10	0.046	0.015	0.219	−0.340	2	0.082

Note: * Indicates that (at the 5 per cent level of significance) a Wald test rejects the proposition that all estimated coefficients for a subject equal zero.

is verified by Wald tests. Table 8.3 provides the corresponding econometric estimates for those subjects where the parameter restrictions imposing symmetry are statistically supported.

In order to build intuition take subject P7 as an example: facing the pattern 1111 (0000) this subject expects a one (zero) to materialize in the next period with a probability of 0.811. Hence, this subject expects runs to continue. When confronted with 101 (010) the subjects expects a one with probability of 0.362 (0.638). Again, the subject expects a continuation of a pattern, specifically here a zigzag pattern.

Table 8.3   Individual models with parameter restrictions for symmetry of pattern responses

Pattern Subject	11/111/1111/ 11111	01/101/0101/ 10101	0/00/000/0000/ 00000	10/010/1010/ 01010	n	R^2
E3	0.080	−0.150	−0.080	0.150	4	0.054
E4	0.019	−0.173	−0.019	0.173	4	0.178
E5	0.093	−0.357	−0.093	0.357	3	0.161
E6	−0.312	−0.232	0.312	0.232	5	0.270
E9	0.281	0.000	−0.281	0.000	4	0.298
F4	0.156	−0.007	−0.156	0.007	3	0.466
F5	−0.375	−0.071	0.375	0.071	5	0.136
F6	0.040	0.018	−0.040	−0.018	2	0.000
F7	0.200	0.113	−0.200	−0.113	2	0.394
F8	0.211	−0.094	−0.211	0.094	2	0.242
F10	0.206	−0.033	−0.206	0.033	2	0.333
P1	−0.416	−0.071	0.416	0.071	5	0.081
P3	−0.318	0.200	0.318	−0.200	4	0.129
P4	−0.022	−0.150	0.022	0.150	4	0.081
P5	−0.249	−0.232	0.249	0.232	3	0.174
P7	0.311	−0.138	−0.311	0.138	3	0.410

8.6   PATTERN RECOGNITION AND MARKET PSYCHOLOGY

In this section the developed model of pattern-based expectations is applied to the study of market psychology. With market psychology we mean the view that human judgement concerning the future can be affected by elements other than rational calculation and that these 'psychological' factors lead to fluctuations in prices and quantities. See, for example, Pigou (1927) for an early presentation of this position. Deviations from strict rationality have come to be associated in financial economics with terms like 'animal spirits' and 'sun spots'. Several researchers have modelled speculative markets (mostly foreign exchange markets) by explicitly introducing actors who extrapolate from the past with simple rules. Examples include Frankel and Froot (1986) and De Grauwe and Dewachter (1993). In this section we perform a market simulation in which we apply our estimated individual models of pattern extrapolation instead of using behavioural models with arbitrarily set coefficients. This is in the spirit of Arthur's (1991) call for designing economic agents that act like human agents. Specifically, we investigate the determination of the market price of a lottery. This lottery or share pays one unit of currency in the case that a binary series (representing the fundamentals) takes value one in the next period and nothing if it takes value zero. The objective probabilities of the two outcomes are not known to the market participants. Instead, as in the experiment, agents learn about frequencies. The market model builds on the assumption that all participants maximize expected utility based on a logarithmic utility function:

$$MaxE[U(q_{j,t})] = P^1_{j,t+1}\ln[A_{j,t} + q_{j,t}(1 - p_t)] + (1 - P^1_{j,t+1})\ln[A_{j,t} - p_t q_{j,t}]$$

$$(8.3)$$

Here, $q_{j,t}$ denotes the quantity of shares demanded by individual j, p_t is the price of this lottery, $P^1_{j,t}$ is the subjective probability of the value one and $A_{j,t}$ is income without lottery. After taking the first derivative of (8.3) with respect to $q_{j,t}$ the individual demand function for shares in this lottery can be written as:

$$q_{j,t} = \frac{P^1_{j,t+1} - p_t}{p_t(1 - p_t)}A_{j,t}.$$

$$(8.4)$$

This function indicates that the individual buys the lottery (that is, holds a long position) if the market price is below the individual's subjective probability assessment and otherwise sells the lottery (that is, holds a short position). Based on (8.4) we can derive the price that equilibrates the market. The equilibrium condition – given zero net supply of the lottery – is:

$$\sum_{j=1}^{s} q_{j,t} = 0.$$

$$(8.5)$$

Here, s denotes the number of market participants. Under the assumption that $A_{j,t} = A$ (that is, all subjects have the same time-invariant income) this can also be written as:

$$\sum_{j=1}^{s} q_{j,t} = \frac{A}{p_t(1 - p_t)}\sum_{j=1}^{s}(P^1_{j,t+1} - p_t) = 0.$$

$$(8.6)$$

From this condition the equilibrium market price is immediately found:

$$p_t = \frac{\sum_{j=1}^{s} P^1_{j,t+1}}{s}$$

$$(8.7)$$

This formula indicates that the market price of the lottery is the average of the market participants' subjective probabilities.

The above framework is the basis for the simulation of a market in which the participants of our experiment trade the lottery described. The asset price (p_t) in this fictitious market is found, according to (8.7), by averaging the subjects' responses at every point of time. We define the fundamental price $\tilde{p}_t$ of this market as the price at which a utility-maximizing individual using the correct objective probabilities has zero demand for the lottery. We know that the objective probability of the value one occurring in the next period is 0.45 when the series takes on the value one and 0.65 when the series takes on the value zero (see Table 8.1). Hence, the fundamental price is:

$$\tilde{p}_t = \begin{Bmatrix} 0.45 \text{ if } x_t = 1 \\ 0.65 \text{ if } x_t = 0 \end{Bmatrix}. \tag{8.8}$$

Figure 8.2 presents the calculated series for p_t and $\tilde{p}_t$ and shows two of the features that observers of asset markets claim to be important and that are difficult to reconcile with rational expectations. First, there are times with large deviations from the fundamental price (see Shiller, 1981, for empirical evidence): in the simulated market the mean absolute deviation from the fundamental price is 21 per cent. Also, there is no convergence to the fundamental price over time witnessed by the fact that the mean absolute deviation from the fundamental price is the same in both halves of

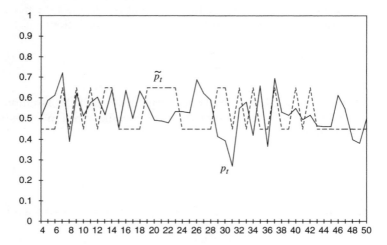

Figure 8.2   Fundamental price ($\tilde{p}_t$) and price based on subjects' responses (p_t)

the experiment. Interestingly, there are not only positive deviations from the fundamental price (as suggested in the literature on rational bubbles) but also negative deviations of an approximately equal size. Second, there are periods when the market price moves without any concurrent change in the fundamentals (see Goodhart, 1990, for empirical evidence): in the simulated market the mean absolute change in p_t over periods with changes in fundamentals is 24 per cent of the average fundamental price whereas in periods without changes in the fundamentals there is still a mean absolute change in p_t of 15 per cent.

Regression analysis can further illuminate the functioning of the described asset market. We first investigate what can account for the variations in p_t. The regression presented as equation (8.9) shows the attempt to capture variations in the market price by variations in the fundamental price. The R^2 of this specification is very low and a Wald test rejects the specification of (8.9) when the alternative hypothesis is that p_t is 0.5 plus noise. This indicates that fundamentals play a negligible role in this simulated market.

$$p_t = 0.478 + 0.092\tilde{p}_t$$
$$R^2 = 0.009,\ SEE = 0.094,\ DW = 2.01 \tag{8.9}$$

Consider the pattern model next. The regressor $\hat{p}_t$ in equation (8.10) is the average of the fitted probability assessments calculated based on those 17 individual pattern models from Table 8.2 that generate (according to Wald tests) significant coefficient estimates:

$$p_t = -0.054 + 1.142\hat{p}_t$$
$$R^2 = 0.204,\ SEE = 0.086,\ DW = 1.939 \tag{8.10}$$

Clearly, the pattern model performs better than the model based on rational assessment of fundamentals. A Wald tests indicates that the coefficient of $\hat{p}_t$ is not significantly different from one and that the constant is not significantly different from zero.

8.7 CONCLUSIONS

This chapter presents a formal model of pattern use in expectations. The model is estimated with individual data gathered in an experiment. This model of pattern-based expectations explains behaviour better than the model of rational expectations. The patterns of runs and zigzag movements appear as particularly important patterns subjects rely on when forming expectations. Estimating statistical models based on the experimental data shows that many subjects rely on patterns in their expectations formation in a systematic way. The individually parameterized models of pattern extrapolation can further be used to simulate market functioning with forward-looking agents. When the calibrated agents are used in the simulation of an asset market we find large and persistent deviations of the market price from the rational expectations fundamental price. Another feature known from real-world financial markets is consistent with pattern-based expectations: price movements also occur in times without innovation in the fundamentals. The next chapter will further pursue how the hypothesis of pattern-based expectations can illuminate the working of financial markets.

NOTES

1. See Rötheli (1998) for elaborations on a model of flexible pattern response involving learning.
2. See Dominitz and Manski (2006) for a position in favour of eliciting expectations in probabilistic form and an interesting application in surveying expectations on pension benefits.
3. Feldman (1963) gave subjects a similar task. In his experiment, subjects were asked to predict the outcome of a binary series one step into the future. He documented qualitatively many of the features regarding the use of visual patterns discussed in section 8.4.
4. See, for example, Kmenta (1971) pp. 174–82.
5. This maximum likelihood estimate of probabilities is tantamount to a Bayesian updating of probabilities provided that a diffuse prior is taken as a starting point. This track is somewhat more awkward but leads to the same answer (see Camerer, 1987, for details).
6. The performance-based pay-off was, on average, also 25 francs. The sum of squared deviations from the optimal probability assessment served as the ordering criterion. The smallest reward paid was 15 francs, while the largest was 40 francs. Only eight subjects of a total of 30 participants preferred the safe 25 francs.
7. The maximum likelihood estimator (choosing the maximum of the posterior density) suggested here as the optimal solution to the problem can be contrasted with the Bayes estimator (choosing the average of the posterior density; see Amemiya, 1994, p. 174). Using this estimator does not alter the conclusions of this chapter. The conclusions of this chapter also hold when we consider the possibility of subjects using either the maximum likelihood or the Bayes estimator based on symmetric, but non-diffuse, priors.
8. There are two practical problems involved in the estimation process. First, it is clear that with the endogenous variable in (8.2) bounded between zero and one the residual of this regression equation cannot be normally distributed. Since for many of the subjects there are entries of $P_{j,t}^1$ that are either one or zero the transformation $\ln(P_{j,t}^1/1 - P_{j,t}^1)$ frequently applied in similar circumstances is not a straightforward alternative here. Instead, we rely on the method of least squares because it yields unbiased parameter estimates even with residuals that are not normally distributed. Given that the efficiency of the least-squares estimates is not granted we do not rely on the estimates of the standard errors for the specification search. Instead, we use the Wald test which does not rely on the assumption of normality of the residual. All tests of significance are conducted at the 5 per cent level.

APPENDIX 8.1 INSTRUCTIONS FOR THE EXPERIMENT (TRANSLATED FROM GERMAN)

You are taking part in an experiment on the formation of expectations by individuals. We will show you a series which can only take on values of one and zero. In every period the series either remains at the same value as in the last period or changes to the other possible number. Your task is to assess the probability of the two possible outcomes for the next period of the series. Hence, your task is not simply to guess the next period's number. Instead, you are invited to give your judgement on the relative likelihood of the two possible outcomes. For every period, you will thus fill in two numbers (which have to lie between zero and one) in the right-hand column of your questionnaire. Please observe that the sum of the two numbers you fill in has to be one. It will be easier to fulfil this requirement if you write your entries as fractions. Observe that the sum of the two numerators has to be equal to the denominator as, for example, **1/2, 1/2** or **1/4, 3/4**. See the following two cases as an example of possible answers:

1. If, after what you have already seen from the series, you judge the two possible outcomes to have an equal probability of being realized in the next period you give the following answer:

1	1/2
0	1/2

This means each value has a probability of 1/2 of being realized.

2. If, after what you have already seen from the series, you judge the value zero in the next period to be realized with certainty then you fill in the table as follows:

1	0
0	1

This means the value one has a probability of zero of being realized and the value zero has a probability of one of being realized.

Extra Information

1. The following is known about the process that has produced the data in this experiment: the probabilities that the values one or zero will be

realized in the next period depend only on the value the series has in the current period.
2. Your financial reward depends on the quality of your answers. The more accurately you assess the probabilities the higher your pay will be. Your answers are of scientific interest even if you make misjudgements. The important thing is for you to make use of the accumulating data as the experiment proceeds.

Procedure

1. You have 15 minutes to think about the task. When you are ready you write down your assessment of the two probabilities for the initial period. Thereafter, you will be given the next value of the series. From then on you have 60 seconds per period to make your probability assessment. The experiment runs over 50 periods.
2. The figure below will serve to record the history of the series.

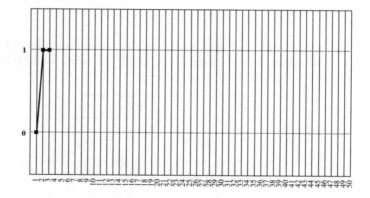

As shown in the above figure the series over the first three periods takes on the following values:

Period	Value
1.	0
2.	1
3.	1

(Here subjects are given a table with a total of 50 periods)
Please start your evaluation of probabilities for period 4:

4.

1	
0	

5.

1	
0	

(Here subjects are given another table that runs through to the 50th period.)

APPENDIX 8.2   THE EXPERIMENTAL SERIES AND MEASURES OF $D_t^{3,i}$

t	Series	$D_t^{3,1}$	$D_t^{3,2}$	$D_t^{3,3}$	$D_t^{3,4}$
1	0	NA	NA	NA	NA
2	1	NA	NA	NA	NA
3	1	0	0	0	0
4	1	1	0	0	0
5	1	1	0	0	0
6	1	1	0	0	0
7	0	0	0	0	0
8	1	0	1	0	0
9	0	0	0	0	1
10	1	0	1	0	0
11	0	0	0	0	1
12	1	0	1	0	0
13	0	0	0	0	1
14	0	0	0	0	0
15	1	0	0	0	0
16	1	0	0	0	0
17	1	1	0	0	0
18	1	1	0	0	0
19	0	0	0	0	0
20	0	0	0	0	0
21	0	0	0	1	0
22	0	0	0	1	0
23	0	0	0	1	0
24	1	0	0	0	0
25	1	0	0	0	0
26	1	1	0	0	0
27	1	1	0	0	0
28	1	1	0	0	0
29	0	0	0	0	0
30	0	0	0	0	0
31	1	0	0	0	0
32	0	0	0	0	1
33	1	0	1	0	0
34	0	0	0	0	1
35	1	0	1	0	0
36	1	0	0	0	0
37	0	0	0	0	0
38	1	0	1	0	0
39	1	0	0	0	0

APPENDIX 8.2 *(continued)*

t	Series	$D_t^{3,1}$	$D_t^{3,2}$	$D_t^{3,3}$	$D_t^{3,4}$
40	0	0	0	0	0
41	1	0	1	0	0
42	0	0	0	0	1
43	1	0	1	0	0
44	1	0	0	0	0
45	1	1	0	0	0
46	1	1	0	0	0
47	1	1	0	0	0
48	1	1	0	0	0
49	1	1	0	0	0
50	1	1	0	0	0

9. Pattern-based expectations and financial markets

9.1 INTRODUCTION

The experimental investigation presented in this chapter builds on the behavioural concept introduced in Chapter 8 and extends the model of pattern-based expectations for applications to time series that are not just binomial. It proceeds on the assumption that at any point in time agents extrapolate (that is, form expectations) based on the specific visual pattern shown by the time series under consideration. Hence, we see agents as 'natural born chartists'. We define a pattern just as in Chapter 8: a pattern is an ordered sequence of length n. Hence, at any point in time the preceding n observations in a time series make up one particular pattern. Thus, every possible combination makes up a pattern and there is no connotation of prominence in this definition of pattern. Hence, according to this definition a series of values – like for example, 100, 101, 101 – constitutes a pattern just as the unbroken upward trend 100, 101, 102 does. An important implication of our definition of patterns is that a question of the sort 'Why do people try to spot patterns in financial data when they are not there?' does not make any sense. A pattern is nothing but the structure of the recent past of a series that is typically perceived by the decision maker in the form of a visual display and that can be coded mathematically as described before. Subjects in the experimental study presented here are not exposed to the expression 'pattern' at all. Instead, what according to definition are patterns of length four are called 'cases of how a series can develop over four periods' in the experimental instructions.

Several researchers in financial economics have already ventured in this direction (see, for example, De Bondt, 1993; Barberis et al., 1998; Bloomfield and Hales, 2002, and Hirshleifer, 2001, for background). Contrary to De Bondt's study our subjects are presented with stylized (not historical) price data. This makes the approach similar to that pursued by Bloomfield and Hales (2002). In contrast to that study, however, we confront subjects with more than a selective list of a few possible sequences in a time series. In fact, the time series in the experiment is simplified to make it possible to represent subjects' responses for all possible recent histories of the time series. We first discuss the behavioural tendencies in response to various patterns and their relevance for financial markets. Here, we document which patterns are behaviourally prominent in the sense of inducing notable and interesting responses. This is taken one step further in an econometric analysis investigating whether the elicited projections can be explained by the model of simple linear trend extrapolation. In this section we show that in the presence of some types of patterns (like trends and zigzag movements) subjects' expectation are indeed qualitatively different compared to expectations in more general circumstances. Finally, the experimental findings are used to model a fictitious financial market. Here, the fact that the experiment asks for price expectations means that the simulated market is a market populated only with so-called 'noise traders' or 'feedback traders'.[1] This section also proposes tests of realism for the proposed model and implements them for the study of exchange rate and stock market data.

9.2 THE EXPERIMENT

In the experiment designed for this investigation (see Appendix 9.1 for the detailed instructions) subjects were shown a time series they were told to consider as a financial price (that is, a stock price or an exchange rate). They were informed that they would see different scenarios of price development over the course of four periods and that it would be their task to assess the likely continuation of this price series.[2] The experiment simplifies the time series which can only proceed in steps of $+2$, $+1$, 0, -1, -2. With this restriction there exist a total of 125 cases of how a series can develop over four periods. The experiment limits the number of cases to 63. This is done on the basis of tests presented in Chapter 8 showing that the hypothesis of symmetry is not rejected for a majority of subjects (that is, agents' forecasts based on a pattern like, for example, -1, $+1$, -1, $+1$ is taken to be the same as that based on the pattern $+1$, -1, $+1$, -1 multiplied by -1). Clearly this assumption could be relaxed but only at the cost of asking subjects to spend more time on the experiment. Figure 9.1 shows the 63 cases (that is, patterns) used in the experiment and numbers them for the purpose of further discussions.

Subjects were given three tasks. Task (a) asks for an assessment of the likely continuation of the series expressed in probability values (in steps of 0.1) for the different possible steps ($+2$, $+1$, 0, -1, -2) of the graph. Task (b) asks for an assessment of the population mean (that is, the average response over all subjects) of the expected values given in task (a). Hence, this task asks for an assessment of the answers by the other

120   *Experiments and applications*

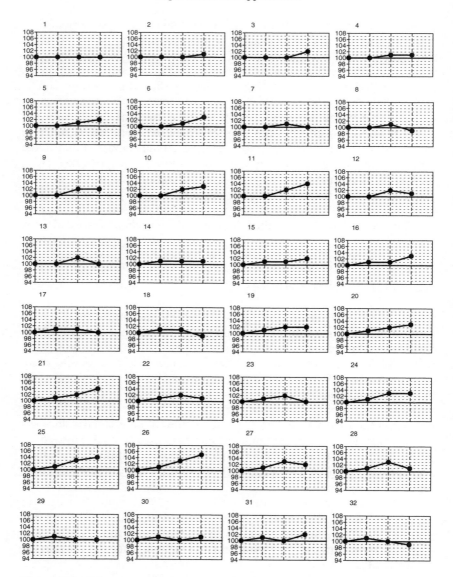

Figure 9.1   The 63 patterns presented in the experiment

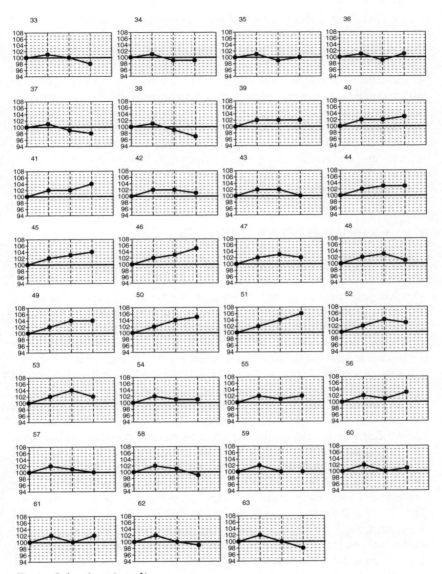

Figure 9.1   *(continued)*

subjects. Here, subjects were asked for a single value between $+2$ and -2 down to one decimal point. Finally, task (c) calls on subjects to express their confidence in their response to task (b). Here, subjects bet between zero and 10 euro cents on the proposition that their answer in (b) differs no more than (in absolute value) 0.5 from the actual mean of the expected values computed over all subjects. Subjects were financially rewarded for participating in the experiment with a show-up fee and a variable payment that depended on the subject's accuracy of judgement and her confidence (see Appendix 9.1 for details). The 45 subjects participating in the experiment were undergraduate students from the University of Erfurt in Germany who had completed at least one principal course in economics prior to the experiment.

9.3   EXPERIMENTAL RESULTS

The first set of issues addressed with the experimentally gathered data concerns the central tendency and distribution of answers to task (a). The first question pursued here is the following: which patterns, in the mean of the responses, elicit a large deviation from zero? Table 9.1 shows the list of the ten most prominent patterns ordered according to the absolute value of the mean computed from the answers given to task (a).[3] All the patterns rated in the top ten are trends. With only one exception the average expected change in the variable is smaller (in absolute terms) than the last observed change in the series. Hence, there is a tendency for expectations to extend trends but also to attenuate them. The next issue is the opposite question asking which patterns lead subjects on average to expect small changes in the variable. Table 9.2 shows the list of the ten most prominent patterns ranked here. Among the patterns that induce small expected changes there are various zigzag movements, a plateau and a broken upward trend. Statistics for all patterns presented in the experiment (not just the top ten shown in the figures) are found in Appendix 9.2. This appendix also shows the standard deviations for the distribution of the means and thus gives an impression of the heterogeneity of answers over the population of subjects. Overall, the results with regard to population means document that the extent to which changes in the immediate past of a series (in particular the very last observed change) are projected into the future critically depends on the pattern shown by the series over the previous few periods. This helps to explain the result reported in the literature of a relatively low slope coefficient estimated with a large standard error in regressions relating expectations to the lagged change of a series (see, for example, Shefrin, 2005, p. 66). Section 9.4 will document this aspect of the data further with econometric estimates.

Table 9.1   Patterns ranked according to the maximum of the individually expected change

Rank	Pattern #	Average of subjects' expected values	Pattern
1	51	1.365	
2	26	1.249	
3	21	1.189	
4	46	1.109	
5	25	1.093	
6	11	1.074	
7	6	1.058	
8	38	−1.013	
9	20	0.889	
10	33	−0.878	

Table 9.2   Patterns ranked according to the minimum of the individually expected change

Rank	Pattern #	Average of subjects, expected values	Pattern
1	36	0.013	
2	1	−0.031	
3	52	−0.042	
4	12	−0.062	
5	30	−0.082	
6	34	0.083	
7	59	0.102	
8	60	0.116	
9	29	0.123	
10	7	−0.140	

The next topic concerns the probability distribution of the individuals' answers. Here we want to know which patterns generate the densest (Table 9.3) and which patterns generate the most even individual probability distributions (Table 9.4). This means we want to know for which patterns agents' probability assessments are most centered and where they are most even.[4] Again, see Appendix 9.2 for the full set of results. The findings indicate that plateaus and trends stand out as patterns that lead to the most concentrated individual probability assessments. These are the types of sequences in time series that lead agents to be most certain about their forecasts. Broken trends, on the other hand, are prominent when it comes to even individual probability assessments. Hence, these are sequences of time series that lead agents to be uncertain about their own projections of financial series.

Comparing answers to task (a) and task (b) yields further interesting insights. Notably, it is worth considering whether there are any patterns that lead to a bias in expectations in the sense that the average of individual answers is systematically higher or lower than the average of the forecast of the population mean.[5] Table 9.5 shows that zigzag movements and emerging trends feature prominently as patterns where agents' judgements of collective assessments are systematically incorrect. Here, the typical outcome is that agents overestimate the change projected by the average respondent. Hence, subjects often expect the average expectation to vary more than it actually does. Whether this tendency has any effect on market outcomes depends on what drives buying and selling behaviour in financial markets. The market model proposed in section 9.4 takes the individual expectations to determine buying and selling decisions. Under these conditions the bias noted here does not affect price movements.

A third set of issues deals with answers to task (c). Here, it is straightforward to investigate whether the subjects' confidence in betting on the assessment of the population average is justified when measured by the average of cents earned. Table 9.6 shows that plateaus and trends are the sort of patterns where subjects are rightly confident about their social judgement and hence realize large gains. Table 9.7, in contrast, presents the type of patterns that lead to the large losses: zigzag movements and broken trends feature prominently.

9.4   HOW WELL DO SIMPLE EXTRAPOLATIVE SCHEMES EXPLAIN THE ELICITED EXPECTATIONS?

It may be asked whether documenting expectations in a pattern-wise way as presented here offers new insights when contrasted to simple schemes of

Experiments and applications

Table 9.3 *Patterns ranked according to the criterion of densest*
distribution of individual expected changes

Rank	Pattern #	Densest distribution of answers	Pattern
1	1	25.040	
2	20	21.120	
3	51	18.346	
4	14	14.460	
5	26	13.820	
6	5	13.624	
7	38	13.280	
8	21	12.260	
9	61	12.096	
10	50	12.067	

Table 9.4   Patterns ranked according to the criterion of most even distribution of individual expected changes

Rank	Pattern #	Most even distribution of answers	Pattern
1	52	5.960	
2	27	6.140	
3	34	6.406	
4	3	6.440	
5	40	6.540	
6	13	6.548	
7	12	6.599	
8	24	6.820	
9	7	6.820	
10	28	7.042	

Table 9.5   *Patterns ranked according to the maximum (absolute) size of*
the bias in the assessment of the population's expectation

Rank	Pattern #	Bias: difference between averages of answers b) and a)	Pattern
1	41	0.167	
2	30	−0.153	
3	3	0.151	
4	11	0.142	
5	55	0.136	
6	10	0.133	
7	19	0.127	
8	2	0.127	
9	35	0.125	
10	16	0.124	

Table 9.6 Patterns ranked according to the maximum average cent amount earned in the assessment of the population's expectation

Rank	Pattern #	Average amount won (in euro cents)	Pattern
1	1	7.489	
2	20	6.911	
3	21	5.422	
4	14	5.400	
5	46	5.311	
6	5	5.267	
7	26	5.111	
8	29	4.822	
9	25	4.778	
10	45	4.556	

Table 9.7 Patterns ranked according to the minimum average cent amount earned in the assessment of the population's expectation

Rank	Pattern #	Average amount won (in euro cents)	Pattern
1	61	−2.400	
2	31	−1.911	
3	53	−1.422	
4	36	−1.267	
5	23	−1.200	
6	63	−1.133	
7	48	−0.911	
8	47	−0.911	
9	56	−0.689	
10	60	−0.267	

extrapolative expectations like those described in Chapter 5. Concretely, it is interesting to assess how well our experimentally documented expectations can be explained by a scheme of trend extrapolation. Expectations are linearly trend-extrapolative when they can be captured by a weighted sum of past changes in the series to be forecast. If X is the time series shown in the experiment and X^e_{t+1} is the (experimentally elicited) expected value of the series one period into the future, we estimate the following regression equation:

$$X^e_{t+1} - X_t = \beta_0 + \beta_1(X_t - X_{t-1}) + \beta_2(X_{t-1} - X_{t-2})$$
$$+ \beta_3(X_{t-2} - X_{t-3}) + \varepsilon_j, \tag{9.1}$$
$$\text{for } j = 1 \text{ to } 63.$$

Here the first four terms on the right-hand side of the equation make up the part of the experimental data that can be captured by the model of linear trend extrapolation and ε_j denotes the part of the elicited forecast after pattern j that is not explained by the linear extrapolation scheme. Note that the β parameters in equation (9.1) are not indexed according to the 63 patterns. This is what standard trend extrapolation really means: the subject values each of the (last three) changes in the variable under consideration with a constant weight. In the estimates, the population average of the expected change (the first criterion value shown in the table of Appendix 9.2) is used as the left-hand variable in the regression. The following parameter values and statistics are found with the method of ordinary least squares:

$$X^e_{t+1} - X_t = 0.033 + 0.341(X_t - X_{t-1}) + 0.195(X_{t-1} - X_{t-2})$$
$$+ 0.032(X_{t-2} - X_{t-3}) \tag{9.2}$$
$$R^2 = 0.863, SEE = 0.224, DW = 2.173$$

The R^2 indicates that the simple model of linear trend extrapolation captures the experimental data quite well. For the reasons reported in Chapter 8 tests of significance for coefficients are not based on standard errors of individual coefficients but are instead conducted by means of Wald tests. For the coefficients in (9.2) such a test indicates that the weight of the change term $X_{t-2} - X_{t-3}$ is statistically negligible but that the other coefficients are jointly different from zero. Hence, it appears that agents take into consideration only the last two changes of the series. The new estimate incorporating this finding is:

$$X^e_{t+1} - X_t = 0.073 + 0.340(X_t - X_{t-1}) + 0.190(X_{t-1} - X_{t-2}) \tag{9.3}$$
$$R^2 = 0.862, SEE = 0.223, DW = 2.146$$

As we detail next, this simple linear scheme has its limitations as an explanation. An analysis of the errors of equation (9.3) suggests that the linear scheme is an oversimplification: the size of the regression error tends to be particularly large for trends and zigzag movements. Hence, the elicited expectations appear to differ systematically over different types of patterns. This can be further investigated by specifying the extrapolative model to allow for β parameters to differ over classes of patterns. Equation (9.4) presents the estimation results when zigzag movements and trends are considered separately from all other circumstances. Hence, the following equation shows estimates of three sets of β coefficients:

$$X^e_{t+1} - X_t = [0.484 - 0.013(X_t - X_{t-1}) + 0.306(X_{t-1} - X_{t-2})]D^{Zigzag}$$
$$+ [0.436 + 0.300(X_t - X_{t-1}) + 0.128(X_{t-1} - X_{t-2})]D^{Trend}$$
$$+ [0.130 + 375(X_t - X_{t-1}) + 0.109(X_{t-1} - X_{t-2})]$$
$$\times (1 - D^{Zigzag})(1 - D^{Trend}) \quad\quad (9.4)$$

with,

$$D^{Zigzag} = 1 \text{ if } (X_t - X_{t-1}) > 0, (X_{t-1} - X_{t-2}) < 0, (X_{t-2} - X_{t-3}) > 0$$
$$D^{Trend} = 1 \text{ if } (X_t - X_{t-1}) > 0, (X_{t-1} - X_{t-2}) > 0, (X_{t-2} - X_{t-3}) > 0$$
$$R^2 = 0.949, \; SEE = 0.142, \; DW = 2.383$$

The regression results indicate that the parameter values are indeed (and statistically significantly so) different for the three classes of patterns considered. For example, the weight given to the last (lag one) observed change is almost zero in those cases when the series makes a zigzag movement. Hence, here we have an explanation for Shefrin's (2005) finding of large standard errors in regressions relating expectations to the (one-period) lagged change of a series. Moreover, when considering the R^2 values for the different classes of patterns we find that the model of linear trend extrapolation captures least well the subjects' responses after zigzag movements of the series ($R^2 = 0.356$) while the linear approximation is much better for the case of trends ($R^2 = 0.995$) and the remaining circumstances ($R^2 = 0.944$). Hence, our evidence indicates that expectations are not adequately represented by the simple model of linear extrapolation.

What does this finding mean for the applied economist who needs to model expectations? One answer is that the modeller ought to be cautious when using simple linear extrapolation schemes as proxies for expectations. A farther reaching answer is the proposition to relate our subjects' answers to the specific economic series agents are modelled as forecasting. For this approach one has to bridge the gap between the simplified laboratory set-up to situations where agents have to predict a series with increments that are not just zero, 1 or 2 per cent changes. This is left to future research. In the next section we propose another way to make the elicited expectations data fruitful for empirical research.

9.5 A SIMULATED ASSET MARKET AND TESTS OF REALISM

The results presented in the previous sections are suggestive for individual and collective expectations on asset markets. What is particularly interesting, however, is to analyse how agents' acting on observed patterns in asset prices affects the course of financial time series. This section addresses this issue with a simple model of asset price dynamics based on the experimentally gathered data. It is a variant of the research strategy proposed by Zeckhauser et al. (1991). The approach chosen here is a short cut in that we do not model the individual demand and supply of assets (as done in Chapter 8) but instead directly infer the market price from the subjects' probability assessments in task (a). The idea behind this is that we look for price paths that have the characteristic of being consistent with the probability assessment of the subjects. That is, we generate histories of financial prices where the expectations elicited experimentally would be appropriate. This is done by imposing the restriction that for every possible pattern emerging in the data the frequency distribution of the realized price change over the following period is equal to the probability distribution of price changes taken from the average subject in our study. Computationally, this is achieved by: (1) calculating the average probability distribution for the changes in the time series for each possible pattern; (2) selecting a starting sequence; (3) drawing a number from the described pattern-specific probability distribution to find the next period's value of the series; and (4) by repeating this process.

As an example consider the starting sequence takes the four successive values 100, 101, 100, 101 (that is, the changes are $+1$, -1, $+1$). The probabilities (averaged over all subjects) for the five possible changes for the step to the next period are $P(+2) = 0.073$, $P(+1) = 0.253$, $P(0) = 0.207$, $P(-1) = 0.451$, and $P(-2) = 0.016$, respectively. Next, turning to computational procedures, divide the region between zero and one into five sub-regions with borders set at the values 0, 0.073, 0.326 (that is, $0.073 + 0.253$), 0.533 (that is, $0.326 + 0.207$), 0.984 (that is, $0.533 + 0.451$) and 1.00 (that is, $0.984 + 0.016$) and let a random number generator (with an even probability distribution) choose a number between zero and one. If that random number, for example, falls in the region between 0.073 and 0.326 the value for the next change of

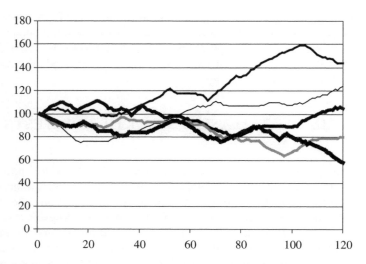

Figure 9.2   Time paths of asset prices simulated on the basis of the pattern model

the series thus chosen is plus one, bringing the series to 102. Continuing the procedure one step further we take the series 101, 100, 101, 102 (that is, -1, $+1$, $+1$) for which the average distribution of expected changes (probabilistically determining the next step) would be $P(+2) = 0.104$, $P(+1) = 0.478$, $P(0) = 0.196$, $P(-1) = 0.182$ and $P(-2) = 0.040$. Again, a random number draw selects the change to be realized next, and so on. The procedure thus stepwise determines a sequence of asset prices. Figure 9.2 shows five randomly selected samples of such time paths simulated with the pattern model of asset prices.[6]

An asset price thus simulated could be termed fully 'sentiment driven' to relate to the title of one analyst's article (Hopper, 1997, 'What determines the exchange rate: economic factors or market sentiment?', p. 17). Given that the model has no role for fundamentals these simulations should be considered a polar case. In order to assess whether the model has any potential for explaining real-world asset price dynamics we evaluate how closely artificial series thus generated resemble actual financial series. For this purpose we generate a large number of time paths of fictitious financial markets and compare them statistically (to be explained below) with the historical series under consideration. As a standard of comparison we generate an equally large number of random walks of the same length as the historical data. The random walk has been a benchmark for empirically assessing models, in particular models that explain exchange rate movements (see Meese and Rogoff, 1983; Cheung et al., 2005, and Evans and Lyons, 2005). The random walk series for our purpose

Table 9.8   Results of exchange rate simulations

Period	1973:01–1982:12	1983:01–1992:12	1993:01–2002:12
Exchange rate			
Swiss franc to Japanese yen	0.5127	0.5646	0.5453
Pound sterling to US dollar	0.5736	0.5149	0.4648
German mark to US dollar*	0.5243	0.5503	0.5158

Note: * Last sample ends in 2001:12 with the replacement of the German mark by the euro.

are generated by taking the average probability answers over all 63 cases given by all subjects and imposing the condition that changes of the same absolute size have the same probability (this restriction is statistically supported). Hence, the steps of the random walk series are drawn from the probability distribution $P(+2) = 0.133$, $P(+1) = 0.234$, $P(0) = 0.266$, $P(-1) = 0.234$ and $P(-2) = 0.133$, respectively.[7]

The realism of the proposed pattern model is judged against the alternative of the random walk model by comparing the simulated time paths (with 120 data points each) from both simulated models to historical financial data. The criterion for comparing the pattern model and the random walk model as explanations of historical prices is the correlation coefficient between the growth rates (first difference of natural logs) of the artificial and the historical series. We count the number of times that the correlation coefficient between the (specific) simulated version of the pattern model and the historical series is higher than the correlation coefficient between the (specific) simulated random walk and the historical series.[8] For every historical series considered we simulate each of the two models 10 000 times and report the relative number of successes of the pattern model. Hence, a value above 0.5 indicates that the pattern model has outperformed the random walk in generating more realistic trajectories whereas a value below 0.5 shows the reverse. The financial series used are: (1) nominal exchange rates; and (2) stock prices of the largest US companies (according to the Dow Jones list). In either case monthly data (generated as end-of-month daily data) covering ten years of data are used.

Table 9.8 shows the results of simulations with exchange rate data. It turns out that in eight of nine sub-samples (with the Swiss franc/Japanese yen, the pound sterling/US dollar, the German mark/US dollar as rates) the pattern model generates a higher correlation of growth rates compared with the random walk alternative in over 50 per cent of cases. Hence, for exchange rates the pattern model appears to outperform the random walk alternative. Table 9.9 shows the results for the ten largest companies listed in the Dow Jones industrial average index. These results show that in the

Table 9.9   Results of US stock price simulations

Period Company	1985:01–1994:12	1995:01–2004:12
Gen Electric Co	0.4664	0.5462
Microsoft cp*	0.4785	0.4955
Exxon Mobil cp	0.4787	0.5172
Wal-Mart Stores	0.5319	0.4906
Citigroup Inc.	0.4982	0.4774
Johnson & Johns dc	0.4829	0.4440
Amer Intl Group Inc	0.4801	0.4964
Pfizer Inc	0.4855	0.5663
Altria Group Inc	0.5383	0.5287
Intel CP*	0.4410	0.5190

Note: * First sample starts in 1987:01.

first ten years investigated (1985 to 1994) the pattern model outperforms the random walk model for only two companies. However, when assessing the period from 1995 to 2004 when (according to analyses like Shiller, 2001) stock prices differed significantly from rational expectations fundamental values the pattern model performs better: for this historical sample the pattern model outperforms the random walk model for half of the stocks considered. Still it appears that for stock prices the pattern model does not outperform the random walk model. How can the difference in success of the pattern model for exchange rates and stock prices be interpreted? One suggestion is the following: in the public discussion on exchange rates there is much diversity in opinions concerning whether and which fundamentals are important for valuing exchange rates. In contrast, when it comes to valuing stocks investors largely agree that future earnings of firms are what ultimately count. This can, for example, be verified by studying views exchanged in so-called message boards on the World Wide Web (see, for example, Antweiler and Frank, 2004). Based on this argument it is not really a surprise to find that a model with pattern-extrapolating noise traders explains exchange rates better than stock prices.

9.6   CONCLUSIONS

The experimental results presented here permit a deeper analysis of pattern-based expectations introduced in Chapter 8. For a simplified time series we experimentally elicit expectations over all possible patterns. We document, for example, which patterns lead subjects to expect a large or small subsequent change in the series and which patterns induce agents to be certain or uncertain about their projections. The econometric analysis of the expectations data shows that time series extrapolation contains important non-linear elements. When a series follows a zigzag pattern subjects tend to forecast in a way that is not well represented by a weighted sum of recent changes. However, when the series follows a clear trend pattern, expectations seem to be approximately linearly extrapolative. The elicited expectations data can also be used as a comprehensive representation of the subjects' expectations. We propose one possibility of using the elicited expectations in empirical work by computing histories of artificial financial prices based on the assumption that markets are populated with pattern-extrapolating noise traders. The simulated financial series suggest that the pattern model holds promise to explain features of financial prices (particularly of exchange rates) that have been difficult to explain with models based on economic fundamentals.

NOTES

1. See, for example, Shleifer and Summers (1990). The notion that our simulated markets are only populated by noise traders means that here agents are not seen to be considering one or several possible structural models of the value of an asset. See Hong and Stein (2003) for a recent effort in that direction. As will be discussed later in the chapter the model of pattern-based expectations could well be combined with the notion that agents form expectations regarding fundamentals. For example, it would be straightforward to consider the implications of pattern-based dividend expectations in conjunction with a model of fundamental valuation.

2. The length (four) of sequences shown was chosen based on the finding reported in Chapter 8 that a majority of subjects' assessments is based on such short patterns.

3. The mean reported here is calculated as

$$\frac{1}{45}\sum_{i=1}^{45} SE_i,$$

where SE_i (S stands for subjective) is the mean of a subject's answer under task (a). For the ranking of patterns the absolute value of the mean is evaluated.

4. The criterion used for this purpose is

$$D = \sum_{i=1}^{45}\sum_{j=1}^{5} (p_j - 0.2)^2,$$

where p_j are the individuals' probability entries for each possible step of the series. The densest distribution is the one maximizing this criterion while the most even distribution is the one minimizing this criterion.

5. Bias for a particular pattern is defined as

$$B = \frac{1}{45}\sum_{i=1}^{45} SE_i - \frac{1}{45}\sum_{i=1}^{45} CE_i,$$

where SE_i (*S* stands for subjective) is the subject's answer under task (a) and CE_i (*C* stands for collective) is the subject's mean of answer under task (b). For the ranking of patterns the absolute value of *B* is used.

6. These paths are generated by first running each history for 180 periods, then leaving out the first 60 periods and setting the starting value of all paths to 100.

7. Clearly, this is a special case of a random walk. However, it is a reasonable competitor for the pattern-based model since it uses the same discrete steps and it does not rely on information of actual financial data (as, for example, an estimate of the variance of the growth rate of an exchange rate).

8. This is tantamount to comparing the R^2 s in regression equations relating the change of the historical series to a constant and the change in the simulated series.

APPENDIX 9.1 INSTRUCTIONS FOR THE EXPERIMENT (TRANSLATED FROM GERMAN)

You are participating in an experiment investigating the forming of expectations on financial markets. Hence, think of the data shown to you in the experiment as stock prices or exchange rates. In what follows you are presented with 63 cases of how the price of an asset (like a stock or a currency) can develop over four periods. The experiment is simplified inasmuch as only the five following steps are possible:

- An increase by 2 (that is, a change by + 2).
- An increase by 1 (that is, a change by + 1).
- No change (that is, a change by 0).
- A decrease by 1 (that is, a change by −1).
- A decrease by 2 (that is, a change by −2).

It is your task in this experiment to forecast the development for the fifth period for all 63 cases presented to you. This means (this is task a) that you have to assign probability values to the different possibilities of the continuation of the displayed path (+ 2, + 1, 0, −1, −2). Please select probability values in steps of 0.1 and note that the sum of the probabilities must equal 1. By way of an example you see below three of many possible answers:

1. example

+ 2	0.1
+ 1	0.2
0	0.4
− 1	0.2
− 2	0.1

In addition, we would like to obtain your estimation of the average of the forecasts of all test persons taking part in the experiment here today for each of the 63 cases (this is task b). This means that you are asked to estimate the forecasts of the other test persons as accurately as possible. Specifically, we are asking you for a single value between + 2.0 and − 2.0 down to one decimal point. The following will give you a hint of a possible procedure to solve this task. Start with your own expected value (your expected value

2. example

+ 2	0
+ 1	1.0
0	0
− 1	0
− 2	0

3. example

+ 2	0
+ 1	0
0	0.5
− 1	0.5
− 2	0

of the change of the displayed variable is the sum of the possible changes weighted with their probability values as given by you) in task (a). In the three examples above this would be 0 (ex. 1), + 1 (ex. 2) and −0.5 (ex. 3). Now predict the average of the expected values of all test persons in (a) and write down this value. If you, for example, in this position enter a value of 1.2 while your personal expected value is 0 (as in example 1 of the possible answers) you judge the average of forecasts to be significantly above your personal forecast.

You will receive, as a financial compensation, a basic fee of 4 euros. For answers to tasks (a) and (b) you additionally earn 10 euro cents per case (that is, a maximum of 6.30 euros). Moreover, we would like to measure the degree of your confidence regarding your answer in task (b). In this part of the experiment you can gain, or lose, money. Specifically (this is task c), we want to know how much (between 0 and 10 cents) you bet on your assessment in (b) being no more than 0.5 above or below the actual average of all subjects' expected values in (a). If your assessment is within a range of 0.5 of the average, you will gain the amount you enter in (c). However, if your assessment deviates by more than 0.5 you lose this amount. Thus, your final pay-off consists of the participation fee of 4 euros and between 0 cents and 20 cents per case.

Case 1:

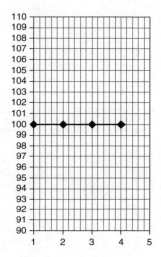

(a) your personal probability forecast (down to one decimal point)

Change	Probability
+2	
+1	
0	
−1	
−2	

(b) your assessment of the average of the expected values of all test persons (down to one decimal point)

....

(c) the amount you bet on your assessment of the average forecast of the test persons (figure without decimal points between 0 and 10)

....

APPENDIX 9.2 CRITERION VALUES AND RANKINGS FOR ALL PATTERNS PRESENTED

Criterion	Average of subjects' expected values			Densest distribution of answers		Bias: difference between averages of answers (b) and (a)		Average amount won (in euro cent)		
Pattern #	C. value	(S.D.)	Rank†	C. value	Rank	C. value	Rank†	C. value	(S.D.)	Rank
1	−0.031	(0.31)	62	25.040	1	0.098*	19	7.489	(5.70)	1
2	0.473	(0.39)	27	8.540	35	0.127**	8	3.356	(5.64)	21
3	0.698	(0.55)	18	6.440	60	0.151*	3	0.822	(5.20)	43
4	0.284	(0.31)	45	8.511	37	0.078	25	3.733	(4.74)	16
5	0.760	(0.36)	15	13.624	6	0.025	52	5.267	(3.90)	6
6	1.058	(0.63)	7	10.960	19	0.100	18	3.822	(5.26)	15
7	−0.140	(0.34)	54	6.820	55	−0.007	60	2.333	(5.54)	27
8	−0.636	(0.50)	20	7.160	53	−0.058	34	0.156	(4.75)	51
9	0.553	(0.52)	23	7.304	50	0.016	54	2.289	(5.29)	28
10	0.596	(0.46)	21	7.500	47	0.133**	6	2.444	(5.14)	26
11	1.074	(0.67)	6	11.162	16	0.142**	4	3.533	(5.76)	17
12	−0.062	(0.61)	60	6.599	57	−0.069	29	2.156	(4.30)	30
13	−0.316	(0.47)	42	6.548	58	0.025	51	0.689	(4.63)	46
14	0.147	(0.25)	52	14.460	4	0.036	47	5.400	(4.83)	4
15	0.443	(0.37)	31	10.105	27	0.111*	12	3.978	(5.29)	14
16	0.802	(0.56)	13	7.920	44	0.124**	10	2.867	(5.07)	24
17	−0.436	(0.47)	32	7.707	46	0.009	59	2.000	(4.63)	31
18	−0.663	(0.61)	19	7.924	43	−0.104	16	0.956	(5.23)	41
19	0.375	(0.37)	38	8.539	36	0.127***	7	3.489	(4.73)	18
20	0.889	(0.31)	9	21.120	2	0.029	50	6.911	(4.57)	2

21	1.189	(0.46)	3	12.260	8	0.029	49	5.422	(4.56)	3
22	−0.196	(0.43)	48	7.220	51	−0.018	53	0.978	(4.70)	40
23	−0.500	(0.74)	25	8.058	42	−0.016	55	−1.200	(4.64)	59
24	0.436	(0.46)	33	6.820	56	0.064	31	2.711	(4.48)	25
25	1.093	(0.46)	5	10.100	28	0.000	63	4.778	(4.91)	9
26	1.249	(0.59)	2	13.820	5	0.080	24	5.111	(5.36)	7
27	−0.147	(0.56)	53	6.140	62	−0.056	37	0.822	(4.39)	44
28	−0.358	(0.70)	39	7.042	54	−0.036	45	0.200	(4.78)	50
29	0.123	(0.22)	55	10.156	26	0.035	48	4.822	(4.22)	8
30	−0.082	(0.58)	59	11.380	14	−0.153**	2	1.422	(5.84)	35
31	0.320	(0.75)	41	7.183	52	0.093	21	−1.911	(5.03)	62
32	−0.424	(0.64)	35	11.860	11	−0.118	11	0.600	(6.37)	47
33	−0.878	(0.57)	10	8.420	38	−0.082	23	0.867	(6.02)	42
34	0.083	(0.34)	58	6.406	61	0.015	56	3.378	(4.05)	20
35	−0.174	(0.67)	51	8.294	40	0.125*	9	0.778	(4.67)	45
36	0.013	(0.72)	63	8.300	39	−0.060	32	−1.267	(4.30)	60
37	−0.482	(0.63)	26	9.380	32	0.058	35	0.600	(5.26)	48
38	−1.013	(0.80)	8	13.280	7	−0.107	14	3.000	(5.09)	23
39	0.288	(0.45)	44	11.102	18	0.076	26	4.400	(5.13)	11
40	0.567	(0.44)	22	6.540	59	0.071**	27	1.889	(5.48)	32
41	0.729	(0.43)	17	11.300	15	0.167***	1	1.222	(6.03)	37
42	−0.316	(0.51)	43	7.433	49	−0.050	40	1.444	(4.83)	34
43	−0.337	(0.79)	40	10.830	21	−0.097	20	−0.111	(4.98)	53
44	0.258	(0.46)	46	10.280	24	0.044	42	2.267	(5.63)	29
45	0.869	(0.36)	11	11.718	12	0.056	36	4.556	(4.44)	10
46	1.109	(0.46)	4	11.405	13	0.100*	17	5.311	(4.29)	5
47	−0.461	(0.65)	29	7.456	48	−0.046	41	−0.911	(4.55)	56
48	−0.400	(0.67)	36	7.744	45	−0.054	39	−0.911	(4.72)	57

Criterion	Average of subjects' expected values			Densest distribution of answers		Bias: difference between averages of answers (b) and (a)		Average amount won (in euro cent)		
Pattern #	C. value	(S.D.)	Rank†	C. value	Rank	C. value	Rank†	C. value	(S.D.)	Rank
49	0.446	(0.66)	30	9.685	30	0.092	22	1.222	(5.33)	38
50	0.861	(0.60)	12	12.067	10	0.013	57	3.111	(5.31)	22
51	1.365	(0.64)	1	18.346	3	0.000	62	4.222	(6.93)	12
52	−0.042	(0.53)	61	5.960	63	0.011	58	1.356	(4.35)	36
53	−0.386	(0.84)	37	10.358	23	−0.054	38	−1.422	(4.77)	61
54	0.191	(0.32)	49	9.500	31	0.042	43	4.022	(3.95)	13
55	0.191	(0.67)	50	8.139	41	0.136	5	−0.067	(5.33)	52
56	0.207	(0.66)	47	8.739	34	0.040	44	−0.689	(5.11)	55
57	−0.471	(0.50)	28	11.120	17	−0.036	46	1.889	(5.35)	33
58	−0.746	(0.76)	16	8.899	33	−0.067	30	0.267	(5.73)	49
59	0.102	(0.45)	57	10.707	22	0.104**	15	3.422	(4.47)	19
60	0.116	(0.56)	56	9.920	29	0.107*	13	−0.267	(4.91)	54
61	−0.541	(1.01)	24	12.096	9	0.006	61	−2.400	(4.60)	63
62	−0.431	(0.58)	34	10.179	25	0.060	33	1.111	(5.38)	39
63	−0.767	(0.85)	14	10.920	20	−0.071	28	−1.133	(5.88)	58

Notes:

† ranking is based on absolute value of criterion.

* significant at 10% level.

** significant at 5% level.

*** significant at 1% level.

Tests for significance only reported for bias measure.

10. Anticipation and coordination failures

10.1 INTRODUCTION

This chapter addresses the difficulties of coordination of investments when decisions have to be based on anticipations of others. It has long been recognized that the successes of entrepreneurs in coordinating their projects with other entrepreneurs is a key factor for both their own success and the aggregate level of economic performance.[1] More recently, theorists have made progress in clarifying the particular problem posed to firms by complementarities in investment when decision making is decentralized (see, for example, Richardson 1959; Haltiwanger and Waldman, 1989; Cooper 1999). In situations where firms do not know each other, or where firms choose for strategic reasons not to inform others or where firms simply do not trust announcements of others, investments, instead of following from contractual agreements, are determined period by period, by an interaction of firms' aims and their conjectures and anticipations regarding other firms' actions. As Richardson (1959, p. 232) writes: 'We seem therefore to be involved in the old difficulty; no one can decide upon his optimal activity without knowledge of what others (who are in the same difficulty) will do.'[2] Experimental analyses of such coordination problems have so far largely been based on the so-called 'stag hunt' problem first suggested as a model of social interaction by Rousseau (1755). Here are the essentials of the stag hunt problem: if an individual hunts a stag (that is, a deer) he needs a partner to succeed. By himself, that is without the help from a fellow hunter, an individual can chase and catch a rabbit. But clearly a rabbit is worth less than (half) a stag. Put into the form of a pay-off matrix the game of stag hunt can be exemplified numerically as shown in Table 10.1.

Here, the respective numbers on the left indicate the pay-off for hunter I while the numbers on the right pertain to hunter II. The equilibrium where both players choose to go stag hunting is pay-off dominant (it gives ten units to each player). Hence, it might be presumed that players generally choose (that is, coordinate on) this Pareto dominant outcome. However, experiments document that empirically this is often not the case (see Van

Table 10.1   The pay-off matrix for the game of stag hunt

Hunter II / Hunter I	Stag	Rabbit
Stag	10, 10	0, 5
Rabbit	5, 0	5, 5

Huyck et al., 1990, 1991, and Skyrms, 2003, for a survey). A key reason for this coordination failure is seen in the fact that without prior communication players' decisions are made under strategic uncertainty: if there is a risk that the other player does not choose (that is, participate) to hunt for a stag it may be better for the decision maker to go after the more modest and safe prey.[3]

The experiment discussed in this chapter goes beyond the stag hunt prototype. The game proposed here is conceptually much richer and hence more demanding for the decision maker than the stag hunt. Output here is the result of physical investments at two different locations.[4] The model world introduced here is realistic albeit highly simplified. Simple laws of geometry, physics and biology determine how investments interact to determine output. This design makes finding the optimal strategy a cognitively demanding task. Our analysis will illustrate how, with decentralized decision making and with the lack of communication, the intellectual task of agents becomes more demanding and how, as a result, performance decreases.[5]

The game is experimentally studied in two versions. In treatment A just one subject controls the investment decisions pertaining to both locations. In this treatment there is no problem of anticipating the actions of another player. In this treatment subjects quickly and fully master their task and the realized level of output is very close to the level predicted by theory. In treatment B decisions are made by two agents who cannot communicate and who decide based on anticipations regarding the choices of the other player. Here, subjects' performance falls far short of the outcome under centralized decision making as well as short of the theoretical ideal. The shortfall of performance in the case of anticipation-based coordination is primarily due to two reasons: (1) decision makers in the decentralized set-up have to solve distributional conflicts such as cost sharing that do not arise in the case of centralized control; and (2) subjects in the situation of decentralized decision making are so absorbed with anticipating the moves of their counterpart that they fail to realize mutually beneficial strategies. As it turns out, losses from the lack of coordination are substantial.

10.2   THE GAME AND THE TWO TREATMENTS

The experiment analysed in this chapter is fairly complicated. It can be understood best when following the instructions as given to subjects. In addition to the written instructions subjects were given a simple cardboard model with which they could build and understand the structures described in the instructions. An experimental instructor assisted the individual subject with the cardboard model for the 20 minutes that were given before the actual experiment started. The written instructions (translated from German) were as follows.

General Part of the Instructions

Imagine a water channel which provides the opportunity to grow a valuable water plant. However, the plant only grows when it is protected from the sun. Sun rays hit the water at right angles. Shade can be generated by protective plates that can be purchased at a price of four money units (called thalers). These plates come in only one version: they are: (1) rectangular; (2) twice as long as wide (two distance units by one distance unit); (3) their length corresponds to the width of the channel. Given these parameters, a single plate cannot cover the channel. Instead, plates on the opposite sides of the channel need to be placed such as to support each other. Figure 10.1 shows the spatial set-up: plates are delivered to a production base (between 1 and −1) by way of an approach road free of charge. Plates can only be placed (and later erected) at identified and numbered slots and they can be ordered and erected

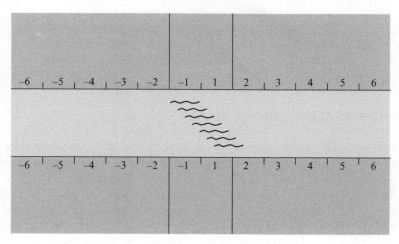

Figure 10.1   The spatial set-up

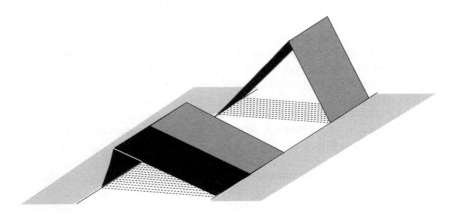

Figure 10.2   A three-dimensional display of modules of a roof structure

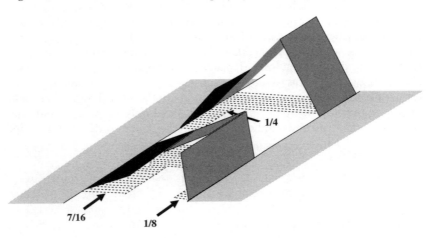

Figure 10.3   Several additional possible roof modules

either vertically or horizontally. This is shown in the three-dimensional display of Figure 10.2, which shows two (of several) possible ways to roof the channel (for contrast the plates are coloured black and grey).

There are several ways to roof the channel that will not shade the entire width of the channel. Figure 10.3 presents several possibilities. The harvest (and the pay-off) for such partial solutions is proportional to the size of the shaded area. If a plate is placed horizontally on one side of the channel and another (single) plate is placed vertically on the opposite side of the channel, the unsupported part of the horizontally placed plate shades a fraction of the channel width. Specifically, according to the Theorem of Pythagoras on right-angled triangles, it provides shade to one-eighth of the channel width. This is indicated in Figure 10.3 by the number 1/8 and an arrow pointing to the relevant shaded area. Moreover, it is feasible (and leads to partial shading of the channel) to lean plates onto other plates on the same side of the channel provided that the latter are supported from the other side. Specifically, a plate X can be placed horizontally so that half of it rests on a plate Y that is placed vertically. If that plate Y comes to rest on a plate Z on the other side of the channel then one-half of plate X also provides shade. Again, only part of the channel is shaded and the extent of the harvest-producing area depends on whether plate Z on the other side is placed vertically or horizontally. In the former case the shaded area is smaller (one-quarter of the channel width, see the upper right module in Figure 10.3) than in the latter (seven-sixteenths of the channel width, see lower left module in Figure 10.3). Again numbers and arrows indicate the respective areas in the figure.

Here are further important points to be noted. If the plates are moved (in discrete steps) to the left or the right of the base, transportation costs are incurred. Moving plates costs two thalers per unit of distance (that is, one width of a plate). Figure 10.4 shows several examples for locations of plates (before mounting) and the corresponding costs. The harvest from an area the size of a square of one distance unit (half the size of a plate) of shaded water is worth 8 thalers. Plates last just one period. The range where plates can be placed extends from +10 to −10. Production is repeated for 20 periods.

Continuation of Instructions for Treatment A (the Centralized Version)

You start with an endowment of 300 thalers and earn or lose money every period of the game. At the beginning of a period you indicate the plates on both sides of the channel you wish to purchase as well as their locations. Then, the plates are simultaneously erected and the shaded area of the channel is determined. You will be informed of the harvest outcome which is computed by a computer program. According to the shaded area you receive the value of the harvest minus the costs for the purchase and transport of plates. If you lose all your thalers the experiment is terminated and you receive no financial reward. One thaler is worth 2.5 euro cents.[6] In every period you may acquire between zero and 20 plates.

Continuation of Instructions for Treatment B (the Decentralized Version)

You start with an endowment of 150 thalers and earn or lose money every period of the game. At the beginning of every period you indicate the plates

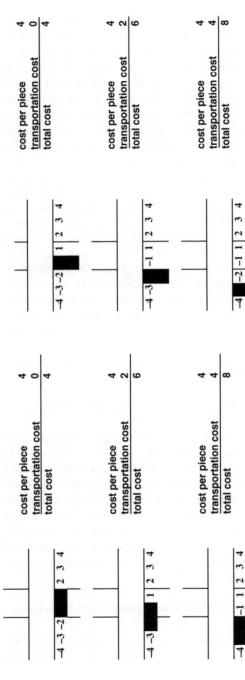

Figure 10.4 Location of plates and costs

on your side of the channel you wish to purchase as well as their locations. At the same time the player on the other side of the channel makes his decisions concerning plates. Then, the plates are simultaneously erected and the plates that come to rest on other plates form a roof. The other plates are lost. The shaded area of the channel is then determined. You will be informed of the harvest outcome which is computed by a computer program. According to the shaded area, you receive the value of the harvest minus the costs for the purchase and transport of plates. You are entitled to the harvest from the middle of the channel to your side of the channel. Hence, it makes no difference whose plate (yours or your neighbour's) provides the shade on your side of the channel. At the end of a production period all the plates (including those that are lost) are observed by both players. If you lose all your money the experiment is terminated and you receive no financial reward. If your neighbour runs out of thalers the experiment is terminated and your thalers are exchanged: one thaler is worth five euro cents. In every period you may acquire between zero and ten plates.

This completes the description of the instructions. Appendix 10.1 describes the computer program used in the experiment and shows examples of the displays presented to the subjects. As indicated, subjects involved in treatment B are provided with the harvest and cost information of both players at the end of every period.

10.3 OPTIMAL STRATEGIES

The basic unit of an efficient way to roof the channel is the module displayed in Figure 10.5. This basic module costs 12 thalers not accounting for transportation costs which vary with its location. In the example of the central location shown in the figure there are no transport costs. The display shows the situation in a two-dimensional presentation before the plates are erected. It is the same module as previously shown (on the left side) in Figure 10.2. Compare this module with a structure where both players place plates vertically (the structure on the right side of Figure 10.2). In this case it takes two such structures (that is, four plates costing a total of 16 thalers) to generate a harvest worth 32 thalers. Compared to the structure built with three plates this structure is not efficient since it generates the same harvest at a higher cost.

How should a decision maker who makes the investments on both sides of the channel conduct his operations? The answer is simple: the decision maker has to evaluate how big a structure based on the efficient module should be built. This means he has to balance additional gains against the cost of plates and the cost of transportation. This is a straightforward optimization

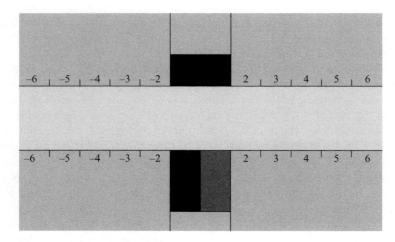

Figure 10.5   The basic module of the efficient roof structure

problem under certainty. It turns out that with the given parameters total net income is maximized when the efficient module is replicated either three- or fourfold around (that is, as close as possible to) the production base. Given the parameters the extra output of the larger structure (four efficient units) is just eaten up by the extra transportation costs. The maximum achievable total net output per period is 40 thalers. Given that there are different cost-equivalent ways to arrange the single modules, there are altogether 48 ways to realize the maximum income. The rational central decision maker implements one of these structures and earns 800 thalers over the course of the experiment.

In treatment B (with decentralized decision making) there are two decision makers instead of one. Each is the owner of one location and the two agents cannot communicate. How should two rational players conduct their operations? The starting point is the same as for a single player. However, not all of the 48 output-maximizing structures described before have to be considered here. Many of the possible structures are afflicted with a social conflict that is visible in Figure 10.5. Here, one player incurs twice the cost of the other player while both players realize the same level of harvest. However, this dilemma can be resolved. The conflict between players is avoided if both sides build their roof structures as an asymmetric mirror image. Figure 10.6 shows one such egalitarian roof structure of the optimal size. It is one of four equivalent structures, which yield a net income of 20 thalers per period and player. Limiting possible choices to these four structures is justified, since a rational agent is one who attempts

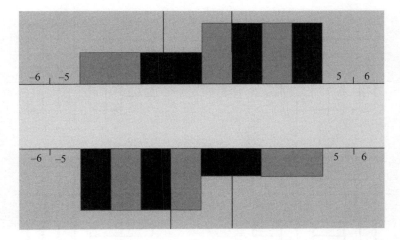

Figure 10.6   An output-optimizing egalitarian and efficient roof structure

to maximize his income under the assumption that his neighbour does the same.

Can the two independent players coordinate on one of these four structures without prior communication of plans? Clearly, a perfect fit of plans is not a matter of certainty. However, there exists an optimal randomized strategy that quickly (in expected terms) leads the two agents towards the optimum. This strategy stochastically dominates the best non-random strategy when the game is played for more than just a few periods. The proof for this assertion can be found in Appendix 10.2. Since rational players – upon reflection of their situation – will both choose this random strategy it can be termed the rational expectations outcome. Contrary to Bryant (1983), this rational expectations strategy is unique. The optimal randomized strategy consists of an initial arbitrary choice of one of the four alternatives on the lower border of the channel displayed in Figure 10.7 (in four panels). With a probability of one-quarter the strategies thus chosen fit optimally and gross output is 128 (that is, 20 thalers net income per player, see the upper left panel). In this case the decisions are perpetuated until the end of the experiment. In the three remaining possible cases the strategies of the two players do not fit perfectly. With a probability of one-half (realizing the case in the upper right or the lower left of Figure 10.7) a gross output of 96 (that is, 4 thalers net income per player) results. With a probability of one-quarter (realizing the case in the lower right of Figure 10.7) a gross output of 64 (that is, −12 thalers net income per player) results. The second part of the optimal strategy consists of a rule for such mismatches of plans. With a probability of one-half each player adjusts his

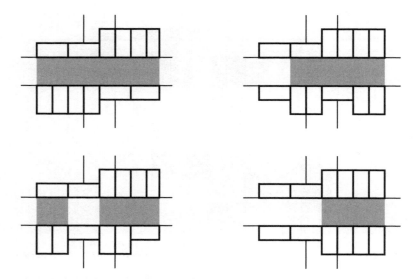

Figure 10.7   The four first-round outcomes with two rational players

choice so as to adjust optimally to the other player's previous choice, and with a probability of one-half he holds on to his choice of the previous period. At every point in time this random strategy has a 50 per cent chance of achieving an optimal fit (in which case choices are perpetuated until the end) and a 50 per cent chance of the output of the previous period being repeated. In the case of a new mismatch the routine of random draws is repeated. In expected terms the resulting net pay-off per player quickly rises over time: the series of expected net output per player is 4, 12, 16, 18, 19 to give just numbers for the first five periods (see Appendix 10.2 for more details). The next section compares the described optimal solutions to the centralized and decentralized decision problem with the actual decisions of human subjects.

10.4   EXPERIMENTAL FINDINGS

Subjects were undergraduate students from the University of Erfurt. Subjects were given either treatment A or B. In treatment A eight subjects were involved while in treatment B eight randomly matched pairs of subjects were involved. We first focus on subjects' performance under centralized decision making (treatment A). Here, all subjects learned to make (no later than in period 8) fully efficient use of their resources. In fact, two of

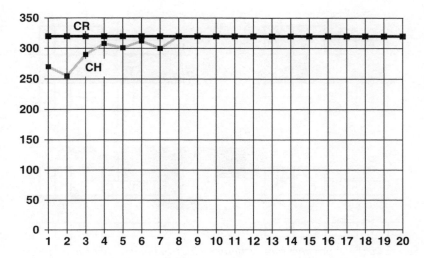

*Figure 10.8   Aggregate net output series for centralized decision making
(CR: Centralized/Rational, CH: Centralized/Human)*

eight subjects implemented the efficient and equitable structure. The remaining six subjects took advantage of the fact that they did not have to find a roof structure that generated equal costs on either side of the channel. In Figure 10.8 the path of net income (summed over all participants) in this treatment is displayed together with the theoretically predicted path with the maximum output achievable. Averaged over periods aggregate income earned is 309.8 thalers which comes close to potential income of 320 thalers.

Contrast these findings with the outcome under decentralized decision making (treatment B). Figure 10.9 shows a typical situation when subjects play the decentralized version of the game. This display again illustrates various ways to place and erect plates. The cross-hatched plates with black frames are plates that cannot be mounted because of lacking support and are thus lost. The shaded areas in the channel indicate where plants can grow protected from the sun.

The optimal strategy described in section 10.3 was not chosen by any of the subjects. More specifically, no subject ever laid down a series of plates that corresponded to one of the four alternatives of Figure 10.7. As a result, no pair of subjects was able to even come close to realizing the full production potential. Figure 10.10 shows production net of costs per period summed over all 16 participants in treatment B. The figure also shows potential output from the optimal strategy as computed in Appendix 10.2,

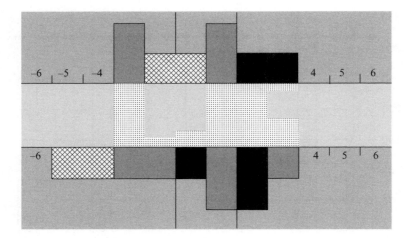

Figure 10.9   A possible roof structure with two boundedly rational players

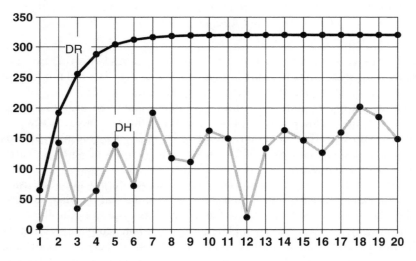

*Figure 10.10   Aggregate net output series for decentralized decision
                making (DR: Decentralized/Rational, DH: Decentralized
                /Human)*

Table 10.A1. Averaged over the 20 periods of the experiment, realized aggregate income (123.4 thalers) is less than half the potential income. An interview at the end of the experiment made it clear that no subject who had
participated in treatment B was able to describe one of the four equitable

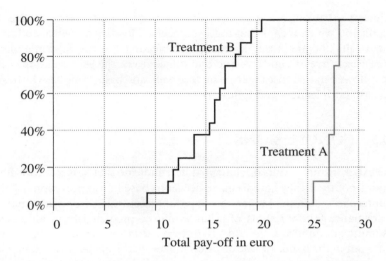

Figure 10.11 Histogram of individual pay-offs in the two treatments of the experiment

and optimally sized roofs. The explanation of this suboptimal behaviour is that in the circumstances captured in this experimental setting the subjects' limited problem-solving abilities combine with the fact that their attention is drawn towards anticipating their neighbours' moves. Hence, little or no time is spent on thinking about structures that would be implemented if the players had a possibility to communicate. Instead, a large variety of different structures were implemented that cannot all be described here. An impression of the heterogeneity is given by Figure 10.11, which displays the distribution of pay-offs in the two treatments of the experiment.[7]

One interesting aspect of behaviour that can be studied more closely is the tendency of individuals to follow others in situations in which decision making is difficult. We search such behaviour by regressing the investment expenses (I) incurred by the individual on his expenses in the previous period as well as on the expenses incurred in the previous period by his neighbour. For each pair of subjects (indexed by i and j) the following pair of regressions is run:

$$I_t^i = \alpha + \phi I_{t-1}^i + \beta I_{t-1}^j$$
$$I_t^j = \varphi + \vartheta I_{t-1}^j + \gamma I_{t-1}^i \tag{10.1}$$

Three cases can be distinguished: (1) no feedback, that is, neither β nor γ is significant; (2) one-sided feedback, that is, either β or γ is positive and significant, which means that one subject is the leader and the other is the follower; (3) two-sided feedback, that is, both β and γ are positive and significant, which means that both subjects are leaders as well as followers. The results document that at least partial feedback is the rule: in a majority of cases (five of eight) we find one subject to be the leader and the other the follower, in two cases there is no feedback and in just one case both subjects are both leaders and followers.[8]

10.5   CONCLUSIONS

The experimental results documented here indicate that subjects coordinate actions poorly if they have to make decisions based on expectations of their counterpart's actions. Under this type of decentralized decision making, performance falls far short of what would be predicted from an analysis assuming unbounded rationality. If, however, decisions are centralized – that is, are put in the hands of one decision maker – subjects perform much more effectively. The main reason for this higher performance is the fact that avoiding coordination difficulties frees attention that is used to search for efficient strategies. With a view to antitrust policy this suggests that in circumstances where coordination is difficult (the coordination of software development and the development of operating systems come to mind), permitting economic centralization may generate output gains large enough to outweigh welfare losses from monopolistic pricing. Microeconomics has increasingly become aware of such possibilities as the chapter on natural monopoly and discrimination in Hey's (2003) textbook documents.

NOTES

1. See Scitovsky (1954) for concepts and several references.
2. Under such circumstances different sets of beliefs (and the corresponding actions) can be mutually consistent. Thus, there is the possibility of multiple equilibria and hence an element of indeterminacy (see Morris and Shin, 2000, for a recent contribution) even when expectations are rational.
3. Game theorists have put much ingenuity into experimentally elaborating various set-ups of the stag hunt and on rationalizing the empirical findings (see, for example, Crawford and Haller, 1990; Crawford, 1991; Battalio et al., 2001). Risk aversion, the size of the premium of the Pareto-dominant strategy, the number of times the game is repeated and the number of hunters (which can be more than two) are some of the important factors.
4. Other types of location problems have been studied as coordination tasks in the tradition of Schelling (1960), for example by Alpern and Reyniers (2002).
5. The set-up proposed here can also serve as a teaching tool for documenting the importance and the difficulties of coordination of plans in economic life: the production process described here is not a black box where everything is simply summarized in a pay-off matrix. Students and non-economists have shown a strong affinity to the tactile nature of the set-up introduced here.

6. The experiment was conducted in 2001 so that the money offered was actually in German marks. The numbers for the exchange rate of thalers to the money paid out have been adjusted accordingly.

7. Figure 10.11 also documents that no subject in treatment B was able to impose a structure on his partner that was exploitative. In principle, a player could organize all his plates horizontally and hope the other player would accept this ultimatum and offer vertically placed plates.

8. In a further treatment not to be discussed here in detail, plates last for two periods instead of just one but plates also cost twice as much and are twice as costly to transport. As a result of these changed parameter values the efficient and egalitarian structures are the same as under treatment B. This variant of the game brings an element of safety into planning. Plates of the other player that are successfully erected can be counted on as existing for one more period and can, if only partially supported, be further built on. In order to have 20 meaningful decisions the game is played for 21 periods in the experiment. The outcome here is very similar to that in treatment B. We find a per-period net output averaged over all subjects of 121.4 compared to 123.4 in treatment B.

APPENDIX 10.1   OUTLINE OF COMPUTER PROGRAM

This appendix gives a brief outline of the working of the computer program developed for the conduct of the experiment. This tool was programmed in Excel and makes use of the logic functions available in the program. Subjects are provided with a paper form in which they can enter their choices, that is, numbers and locations of plates. The upper display in Figure 10.A1 shows how the choices of the subjects are entered into the program. Here we see a case where both subjects purchase two plates. Each plate is represented by two adjoining cells filled with a 1. In general, subjects have the possibility to buy up to ten plates and indicate how they want them to be positioned. The lower display shows the outcomes in terms of harvest, costs and incomes. This visual display of the channel is generated by having the width of the channel split into 16 slices. This is necessary because there are cases where (depending on circumstances) either 2/8, 4/8, 7/8 or 8/8 of one side of the channel are covered by shade. Here, the program tests logically the positioning of the plates on both sides of the channel and identifies whether this slice (that is, one cell) of the channel is shaded or not. If plates do not cover this cell (that is, if no shade is provided) the function active in the cell computes a value of zero. If, however, shade is provided the function in this cell computes a positive value. The impression of shade (or plants) is generated by having the resulting number in the cell in this case equal to 7777777777 and squeezing cells so as only to show the //////////.

Choices:

Player I

Player II

Placement of plate 1

Placement of plate 1

Placement of plate 2

Placement of plate 2

Placement of plates 3 through 10: no further plates purchased

Outcomes:

Player I: Harvest (8), cost (10, two plates for 4 thalers each and 2 thalers for transportation), net money return for this period (2)

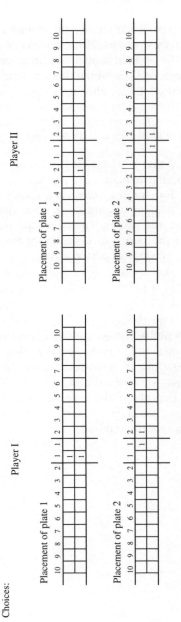

Player II: Harvest (10), cost (12, two plates for 4 thalers each and 4 thalers for transportation), net money return for this period (2)

Figure 10.A1   The display of choices and outcomes

161

APPENDIX 10.2   PROOF THAT OUTLINED STRATEGY IS OPTIMAL

This appendix provides a proof that the randomized strategy described in the text stochastically dominates the (next-)best non-random strategy. We proceed in two steps: first, it is shown that the optimal probability (denoted here by p) of change for the case of mismatch of plans in the random strategy is indeed one-half as asserted in the text. To see this, recall that the expected income in period one is:

$$Y_1^R = 64p^2 + 2p(1-p)128 + (1-p)(1-p)64 = -12 + 64p - 64p^2.$$

Deriving the first-order condition we find that $p = \frac{1}{2}$ maximizes expected income. Second, note that the safe per-period income (Y^{NR}) of the best non-random strategy is 12. This non-random strategy is what a rational player chooses when looking for the best strategy among those strategies where both players do the same. This income results when each player erects four vertically placed plates within the base. In contrast, the per-period income from the suggested random strategy in period n is:

$$Y_n^R = 20\left[1 - \frac{3}{4}\left(\frac{1}{2}\right)^{n-1}\right] - \left(\frac{1}{2}\right)^{n-1}.$$

Table 10.A1 shows per-period income as well as the accumulated income under both the random and the non-random strategy as the total length (in our set-up this is 20 periods) of the experiment increases. Hence, the random strategy offers a larger expected pay-off when the game is played for more than four periods. With the 20 periods of the experiment conducted here the expected pay-off of the random strategy is more than 50 per cent larger than the pay-off of the non-random alternative.

Table 10.A1   *Income under the best random strategy and the best non-random strategy*

Period	Per-period income non-random strategy	Per-period expected income random strategy	Accumulated income non-random strategy	Accumulated expected income random strategy
1	12.0000	4.0000	12.0000	4.0000
2	12.0000	12.0000	24.0000	16.0000
3	12.0000	16.0000	36.0000	32.0000
4	12.0000	18.0000	48.0000	50.0000
5	12.0000	19.0000	60.0000	69.0000
6	12.0000	19.5000	72.0000	88.5000
7	12.0000	19.7500	84.0000	108.2500
8	12.0000	19.8750	96.0000	128.1250
9	12.0000	19.9375	108.0000	148.0625
10	12.0000	19.9688	120.0000	168.0313
11	12.0000	19.9844	132.0000	188.0156
12	12.0000	19.9922	144.0000	208.0078
13	12.0000	19.9961	156.0000	228.0039
14	12.0000	19.9980	168.0000	248.0020
15	12.0000	19.9990	180.0000	268.0010
16	12.0000	19.9995	192.0000	288.0005
17	12.0000	19.9998	204.0000	308.0002
18	12.0000	19.9999	216.0000	328.0001
19	12.0000	19.9999	228.0000	348.0001
20	12.0000	19.9999	240.0000	368.0000

11. Money, transactions and expectations

11.1 INTRODUCTION

The last chapter of this book investigates market transactions and in particular the role played by money. We develop a model of a market economy to examine the role of expectations in the determination of an economy's price level. With this focus the chapter tackles one of the key issues of monetary theory. It is important to clarify from the outset that the economy studied here is fully monetized. This means that all goods have to be paid for with the general medium of exchange. Hence, we do not attempt to explain why the model economy is a monetary as opposed to a barter economy. Hicks (1969, 1989) offers important historical and theoretical arguments for why monetary models should start with descriptions and assumptions regarding the use of money rather than try to incorporate explanations for the use of money. Examples of this type of modelling in monetary economics are Clower (1967), Niehans (1978, Chapters 2–4), Krugman et al. (1985) and Shubik (1990).[1] In the sort of analysis of monetary economies pursued here, the researcher starts the modelling by clarifying the distribution of goods among agents, the agents' preferences, the market form and, in particular, the conventions regarding the timing of market events. A model economy specified accordingly naturally lends itself to experimental analysis.[2] The model detailed in this chapter is such a 'playable' economy and with this set-up we can experimentally study individual rationality and aggregate outcomes.[3]

The key issue addressed here is the determination of the price level in a market economy. It turns out that the model economy studied can operate at different price levels, and expectations play a decisive role in determining money prices. Several strands in the theoretical literature investigate the possibility of price-level indeterminacy. One line of argument goes back to Wicksell (1898) and identifies the policy of interest rate setting as a source of price-level multiplicity (see also Sargent and Wallace, 1975).[4] Another line of argument points to the multiplicity of divergent price-level paths in perfect foresight models (see, for example, Brock, 1975). A multiplicity of stable price-level equilibria in perfect foresight models has been explored by

Obstfeld (1984). A further variant of this topic can be found in an overlapping generations model where, given a path of the money supply, there are two stable price-level paths. With respect to this last version of non-uniqueness of the price level, experimental analysis by Marimon and Sunder (1993, 1994, 1995) has provided some evidence pointing toward one equilibrium, namely the low-inflation equilibrium.[5] The model economy developed here can further be used to study how a market economy reacts to a change in the supply of money. This permits us to assess a central proposition of monetary theory, namely that nominal prices, *ceteris paribus*, move proportionally to a change in the money supply.[6]

11.2 A PLAYABLE MONETARY ECONOMY

The following describes a simple monetized economy. Consider a world populated by an equal number of two types of agents: A-types are assumed to be endowed every period with a fixed amount (100 units) of A-goods while B-types receive 100 units of B-goods per period. While endowments are specialized, both types of agents have the desire to acquire the good that is not in their endowment. This desire is modelled by having each agent i produce a final (consumer) good called C with a production function $C_i = \sqrt{A_i B_i}$. As indicated before, the model economy is a monetized economy. This means that agents buy and sell goods for money. Hence, an A-type wanting to acquire B-goods has to offer money and the same holds for a B-type desiring A-goods. Transactions (a quid pro quo of goods against money) take place in two markets and revenues from sales in one market cannot, within the same market period, be allocated to purchases in the other market. Each subject is initially endowed with an identical amount of cash (100 units). In the basic set-up the aggregate supply of money remains fixed over time. We simplify the selling and buying behaviour by giving agents just one behavioural parameter for each market they operate in: (1) the selling behaviour is determined by agents deciding on the fraction of their commodity endowment they want to sell in each period; (2) the buying behaviour is determined by agents deciding on the sum of money they are willing to spend on the good that is not yet in their possession.

An anonymous market mechanism determines equilibrium prices.[7] The equilibrium price in any market is determined on the assumption that the sum of money offered for purchases is considered to be a unitary elastic individual demand function. This implies that the equilibrium price in a given period is the total of all amounts of money offered for a specific good divided by the total of all units offered of this good. The goods are assumed to be perishable, that is, they cannot be stored. In the experimental application of this model the financial reward of subjects is directly linked to the number of consumption goods produced over the course of the experiment. A positive value of the money held by subjects in the final period of the experiment is ensured as follows: we offer A- and B-goods to the subject in equal proportion in exchange for the remaining cash at the average of the goods' prices in the final period. This implies that subjects receive the maximum possible amount of C-goods for their remaining balances.[8]

Consider first how this economy would function if agents could communicate plans and commit themselves to the agreed plans. Obviously, a situation where each of the market participants offers 50 units of the endowment good and receives 50 units of the other good maximizes output per agent (50 units of consumption goods). If various alternatives could be debated, clearly agents would agree on the described efficient and egalitarian outcome. What is interesting is that this outcome can be engineered (that is, brought about by transactions) in many different ways regarding money flows. Any positive amount of money between zero and 100 is feasible (and leads to the efficient outcome) if every player offers this amount. If agents could communicate and commit themselves they would certainly be able to agree on one number. Hence, in this economy the maximum output of 1000 units of the consumption good can be produced (and the necessary transactions carried out) with very different amounts of money changing hands. This means that the price level in this economy can be anything larger than zero and up to a value of 2 where we understand the price level to be the average of the prices of the A-good and the B-good. Nothing more specific can be said about the resulting price level. Hence, to the extent indicated, the equilibrium price level in the model economy is indeterminate. This indeterminacy similarly holds for the level of real monetary balances and for the level of the velocity of circulation (that is, the ratio of nominal output to the money stock). This form of indeterminacy of the price level is well known and is discussed in the literature as an implication of Say's law (see Patinkin, 1949).[9]

Contrast now the working of our economy when offers cannot be communicated and agreed on among agents. In this situation agents have to form expectations. How should a rational individual behave in this situation? Clearly, the problem investigated here has many similarities with the coordination problem discussed in Chapter 10. Ochs (1995) explores such parallels. This section – without going into a detailed game-theoretical analysis – describes an equilibrium that will serve as a benchmark for the experimental investigation that follows. The equilibrium considered here is based on the notion of unbounded rationality. A thought experiment is helpful for deriving this equilibrium. Consider each of the perfectly rational market participants sitting in a separate room considering the problem of choosing a quantity of endowment goods put up for sale (y_t) and an amount of money (x_t) to be offered for purchases. Imagine this task as choosing two numbers that will be repeated for all periods of the game. Reflecting on the choice of money offered, it can be argued that – given that every number between zero and 100 is equally likely to be drawn if chosen randomly – a rational agent would offer 50 (the expected value) units of money.[10] Given that every agent offers 50 good units, both goods' prices are 1 in the resulting equilibrium. Now if all decision makers choose the strategy outlined (with $x = 50$ and $y = 50$), no subject has a motive to deviate from it because the individual is indifferent between following this particular strategy and any other strategy that shares the feature that the sum of expenses for goods purchased and the number of goods offered for sale is 100.[11] As the theoretical and experimental studies of coordination problems covered in the last chapter indicate, it is not very likely that human decision makers will coordinate on the strategy just outlined. However, for the experimental investigation we can use this perfect-rationality equilibrium as a benchmark.

11.3 EXPERIMENTAL ANALYSIS

We enacted this playable economy as an experiment with students of the University of Erfurt. All participants had successfully completed at least one year of economics courses. The model economy was studied in an anonymous laboratory setting with ten A-type and ten B-type subjects per run of the experiment.[12] Subjects had to make their independent decisions period by period without the possibility of prior communication. Appendix 11.1 shows the detailed instructions. Three such economies, each populated by 20 individuals, were enacted. Subjects were allowed to participate in only one of these economies. Subjects were informed that they would receive 1 euro cent per unit of the consumption good produced. Subjects had three minutes per market period to make their decisions regarding sales and purchases. Before the actual experiment three trial periods were allowed. After this trial phase treatment one was run. In this treatment no external changes impacted on the laboratory economy. All three economies (that is, groups of 20 subjects) started with this treatment. Two groups of subjects were then given treatment two. Under this treatment subjects receive an additional amount of 50 units of money after the end of period 10. From then on the money stock remains on its elevated (by 50 per cent) higher level. Under treatment three (given to one group of subjects after the initial treatment) agents have to deal with endowment uncertainty: here, subjects receive commodity endowments that vary randomly.

Subjects are informed that: (1) their endowments are on average 100 units per period; and (2) their endowments fluctuate in any period with a standard deviation of 10. In treatment three endowments over all subjects were determined so that there is no aggregate risk. That is, in any period total endowment of A-goods and B-goods is 1000 as in all other treatments studied.

11.3.1   Assessing Individual Rationality

We can assess the rationality of individual behaviour by considering the agent's maximization problem. At any point during the experiment the agent maximizes the expected sum of his future pay-offs by an appropriate choice of sales and purchases. The expected sum of pay-offs (denoted by V^e) is:

$$V_t^e = \sqrt{(100 - y_t)\frac{(m_{t-1} + y_{t-1}p_{y,t-1} - m_t)}{p_{x,t}^e}}$$
$$+ \sqrt{(100 - y_{t+1})\frac{(m_t + y_t p_{y,t}^e - m_{t+1})}{p_{x,t+1}^e}} + \dots . \quad (11.1)$$

The variable y stands for the number of goods offered for sale, p_y is the price of this type of (the endowment) good, and p_x is the price of the good that is not in the endowment. The superscript e indicates that decision making is based on the expected value of the respective variable. These expectations must be understood as subjective expectations of the individual agent. Note that at the time of the decision the prices of the current period are not yet known. The variable m_t denotes the level of money balances the individual keeps in period t after offering money for purchases but before receipts from sales in period t have been added. Hence, $m_{t-1} + y_{t-1}p_{y,t-1} - m_t$ is the sum of money spent on purchases in period t. This sum of money expenses is what we abbreviate with x_t. The three dots on the right-hand side of equation (11.1) indicate that, typically, more than just two periods remain over which production takes place. Yet, for the optimization problem for period t the two terms explicitly stated on the right-hand side of (11.1) fully capture the influence of the decision variables m_t and x_t on V_t^e. After deriving the two first-order conditions for the maximization problem the following equation describing optimal choices by the individual can be written:

$$p_{y,t}^e = \frac{m_{t-1} + y_{t-1}p_{y,t-1} - m_t}{100 - y_t} = \frac{x_t}{100 - y_t} \quad (11.2)$$

This optimality condition is used here to infer the price expectation of the individual from his choices (that is, from the data on x_t and y_t).

Intuitively, this procedure can be described as follows: an agent who has gone through the described optimization procedure has chosen a ratio of 'money offered for purchases' to 'goods offered for sale' equal to his expectation of the sales price of the good in his endowment. Hence, his choices reveal his subjective expectation concerning the sales price. Before turning to the statistical assessment of these inferred expectations we perform a basic rationality test. Here is the idea of the test: at any point in the experiment a subject (independent of his price expectation) can rationally decide to abstain from purchasing goods and transfer his money balance to the next period. This option is reflected in equation (11.2). If both sides of this equation are multiplied by $100 - y_t$ we find that one way to establish equality is a choice of $x_t = 0$ coupled with a choice of $100 - y_t = 0$ (that is, $y_t = 100$). This means that with no purchases of the other good, the subject must sell all the goods in his endowment. This is a simple (necessary but not sufficient) rationality requirement. Likewise, a choice of $y_t = 100$ is only rational if no goods are purchased. Buying other goods (that cannot be stocked) is not a rational choice when all endowment goods are sold. Accordingly, for every subject we check whether there are any instances where the described rationality condition is violated. Table 11.1 indicates that over the three runs of treatment one out of a total of 60 participants six subjects (identified by nr for non-rational) violate the described rationality condition at least once.

As a further statistical test of rationality of individual expectations we make a comparison of the forecast performance of the individual expectations derived by (11.2) with the simple scheme of static expectations. More specifically, we document the ratio of the root mean square error of the inferred expectations to the root mean square error of static expectations. A value above one for this ratio indicates that the subject's expectations fared worse than static expectations. Table 11.1 shows the results for the individual subjects. All inferred expectations fare worse than the scheme of static expectations. Considering that the standard of static expectations is a rather weak norm for assessing expectations, this finding is strong evidence that individual expectations are not rational in the present experiment. This finding matches the result from an experimental analysis of a monetary economy by Marimon and Sunder (1995).

11.3.2 Aggregate Outcomes

Here we document the aggregate outcomes from the experiments. Figure 11.1 shows the data for the aggregate realized output in the six runs of the experiment. Figure 11.2 presents price levels and Figure 11.3 displays the real monetary balance (that is, the ratio between the supply of money and

Table 11.1 Tests of individual rationality for treatment one

Subject (types)	1 (A)	2 (A)	3 (A)	4 (A)	5 (A)	6 (A)	7 (A)	8 (A)	9 (A)	10 (A)	11 (B)	12 (B)	13 (B)	14 (B)	15 (B)	16 (B)	17 (B)	18 (B)	19 (B)	20 (B)
Economy																				
1	2.8	12	6.6	2.8	2.5	2.3	2.2	1.6	3.6	nr	2.6	2.9	1.9	1.9	1.8	2.5	3.0	1.9	3.5	7.6
2	4.5	7.0	3.1	2.7	2.0	3.1	3.1	4.2	2.7	2.8	3.8	5.9	1.9	2.8	3.4	3.8	3.8	4.2	4.8	nr
3	4.3	1.9	3.5	nr	4.8	4.1	2.5	1.5	nr	5.1	4.0	nr	2.1	10	nr	4.1	4.2	3.9	4.9	3.7

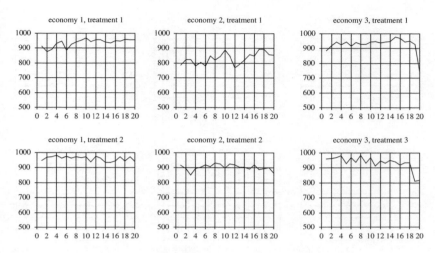

Figure 11.1   Output levels in the six runs of the experiment

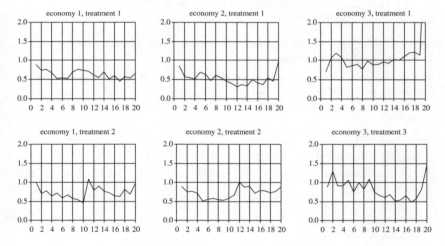

Figure 11.2   Price levels in the six runs of the experiment

the price level) held. Table 11.2 shows the means and standard deviations of these variables. The numbers on total output document that – considering the significant individual choice idiosyncrasies – the market economy manages to generate a rather high level of output. On average over all runs of the experiment we find that output is at 92 per cent of the maximum level of production. This performance is in part due to the precise form of the production function used in the experiment and to the fact that in all runs

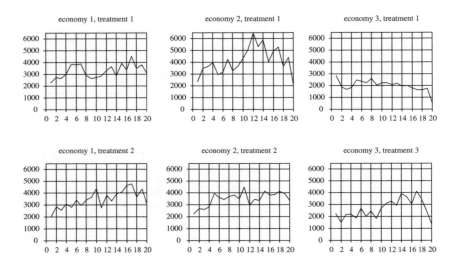

Figure 11.3   Levels of real money balances in the six runs of the experiment

Table 11.2   Statistics for aggregate output and real money balances under different treatments

Economy, treatment	1,1	1,2	2,1	2,2	3,1	3,3
Variable						
Mean Aggregate output	937	960	832	902	928	935
(standard deviation)	(26)	(15)	(38)	(19)	(48)	(45)
Mean Aggregate real money balances	3275	3488	4123	3493	2013	2655
(standard deviation)	(580)	(737)	(1133)	(585)	(476)	(780)
Number of agents with an average of more than 50 units of output per period	10	7	6	9	4	11

of the experiment some traders manage (although not optimally) to take advantage of the prevailing market conditions. The third line of Table 11.2 presents the numbers of players who managed to generate more than the 1000 output units possible in an efficient economy with homogenous agents. Hence, the effect in market economies (stressed, for example, by Friedman, 1953) that some players take advantage of opportunities resulting from other agents' errors and thereby move the market result toward the efficient outcome, is operative here. We note one further result regarding output: endowment risk does not appear to diminish the level of output achieved.

Turning to nominal prices: the realized price level is significantly below the level (of one) predicted based on perfect rationality in two of the three laboratory economies. In one case (abstracting from an apparent end-of-experiment effect) the price level is not significantly different from one. With respect to real money balances the numbers indicate that in all runs of the experiment real cash balances held are above the level suggested by an analysis based on the assumption of unboundedly rational behaviour. In fact, the level of real balances varies widely over the six runs of the experiment. This confirms the theoretical prediction that the market economy studied here – at a given level of the money stock – can operate at different price levels.

11.3.3 Tests of the Quantity Theory of Money

As indicated earlier two groups of subjects were presented with treatment two after the initial treatment. Under treatment two the supply of money is increased (by way of a transfer of 50 cash units to every subject) after the tenth market period. After this expansion the money stock remains on its elevated (by 50 per cent) level for the rest of the experiment. Referring to Figure 11.2 (economies one and two under treatment two) it is apparent that the price level increases after the infusion of money (that is, after the tenth period). The 'quantity theory of money' (see Niehans, 1978, for a detailed description) predicts that the price level changes in proportion to the change in the money supply. One possible test of this proposition is to compare the average price level before and after the change in the money stock. In this perspective the price level for periods 11 to 20 should be higher than in the first ten periods proportionally to the increase in the money stock (that is, 50 per cent higher). When conducting t-tests this quantity-theoretic prediction is supported by the data.

Furthermore, we can assess the prediction of the quantity theory of money by means of econometric analysis. For this purpose, we run a regression of the logarithm of the price level on a constant, a time trend and the logarithm of the aggregate supply of money.[13]

Estimate for economy one (standard errors in parentheses):

$$p_t = -6.735 - 0.040 trend + 0.859 m_t$$

$$(1.501) \ (0.012) \qquad (0.202) \qquad\qquad (11.3)$$

$$R^2 = 0.520, \ SEE = 0.156, \ DW = 1.740$$

Estimate for economy two (standard errors in parentheses):

$$p_t = -6.109 - 0.028trend + 0.762m_t$$

$$(1.392)\ (0.011)\qquad (0.187)$$

$$R^2 = 0.550,\ SEE = 0.145,\ DW = 1.673 \qquad\qquad (11.4)$$

In both economies the coefficient of the money stock is not significantly different from one. A test of a more general specification rejects the proposition of a lag in price-level adjustment: the coefficient of the lagged price level is found not to be statistically different from zero. Hence: (1) as would be predicted from models where prices can be adjusted at no costs the price level in our experimental economy adjusts immediately to changes in the money supply; and (2) this adjustment is quantitatively in line with the quantity theory of money, that is, approximately proportional to the change in the money supply.[14] The latter result is particularly interesting considering the reported strong evidence for bounded rationality of subjects in our experiment. This result suggests that the quantity theory of money may be one of the economic relationships that are robust to agents' deviations from perfect rationality.

11.4   CONCLUSIONS

The analysis of this chapter studies the role of expectations in the determination of the level of nominal prices in an economy. The theoretical analysis of a model economy highlights that a monetary economy can, in principle, operate at many different price levels. Under perfect rationality of agents it is conceivable that a coordination of expectations takes place so as to determine a unique level of nominal prices. Our laboratory analyses document that the experimentally realized price level typically does not coincide with this theoretical prediction and varies over different runs of the experiment. The study further documents that despite a prevalence of individual expectations errors an important result from monetary theory appears to hold: a change in the supply of money leads to a proportional change in the price level. However, the quantitative effect of a change in the supply of money on the price level cannot be assessed very accurately. Therefore, the findings of this chapter should be taken as caveats for a monetary policy that attempts to stabilize the price level by controlling the money supply. Expectations, as our results show, can significantly affect the price level independently of controllable variables.

NOTES

1. This does not preclude that in some of these models payments can be deferred and that credit exists.
2. Duffy (1998) offers a useful survey of laboratory experiments in the field of monetary economics.
3. To clarify the theoretical position taken here with respect to the modelling of monetary economies it should be helpful to contrast this position with its main alternatives. Over the years a great deal of effort has gone into exploring theories that model the use of money in analogy with other goods that are held for the services they provide, and in particular exploring how the holding of money can be justified based on rational choices of agents (see Rötheli, 2006, for a detailed discussion). Important studies analysing the demand for money along these lines are, among others, Keynes (1936), Baumol (1952), Friedman (1956) and Tobin (1958). Among the attempts at deriving money demand from rational choices further important contributions are: (1) Patinkin (1950–51) who proposes to put money holdings into the economic agents' utility function; (2) Dornbusch and Frenkel (1973) who propose money as an argument in the production function; and (3) Samuelson (1958) who explores money as a store of value in an over-lapping generations framework. Many of these approaches (see Kiyotaki and Wright, 1989, 1992, for exceptions) are problematic short cuts: it is questionable to treat the demand for money balances analogously to the demand for TV sets and automobiles. These goods – just like money – provide services sometimes and lead to opportunity costs. However, the analogy is strenuous since money provides its service only inasmuch as it can be given away in return for a good.
4. McCallum (2004) offers a more general discussion and more references regarding the monetary strategies prone to the problem of price-level indeterminacy.
5. These results of these experimental investigations do not directly compare with the present study since they use an overlapping generations model of a monetary economy.
6. We cannot in any meaningful way study the effects of money on output since we have perfectly flexible prices. See Fehr and Tyran (2001) for an experimental analysis relevant for 'real' effects of money.
7. One can think of these markets as operated in trading (or transactions) posts. There, the goods supplied and the amounts of money offered are deposited. Once the equilibrium prices are determined, goods and money are distributed to the respective recipients. Clearly, this set-up also takes care of the solvency requirement. That is, it guarantees that all contracts are honoured.
8. Ensuring that money has a value in the final period of the game is an important aspect of experimental analyses of money (see Duffy, 1998). The specific valuation chosen here attempts to make agents indifferent between spending money in the current period and deferring it to the last period. In the equilibrium assuming perfect rationality discussed below, this indifference holds exactly.
9. In Patinkin's (1949, p. 20) words: 'This was the assumption of Say's law. According to this law the only reason people supply commodities is in order to use the receipts to purchase other commodities. The decision to supply simultaneously involves a decision to spend the receipts. People do not sell to obtain and hold money; money is only a "veil" concealing the true barter nature of the economy. Thus aggregate demand for all commodities must always equal aggregate supply – regardless of prices'; and (p. 21): 'The absolute prices must remain undetermined'.
10. It is arguable whether the expected value (that is, a level of 50 money units offered) can be called a 'focal point' in the sense used in game theory (see, for example, Schelling, 1960, and Sugden, 1995).
11. Call x the expenses for goods purchased (considering the unitary price this is also their number) and y the number of goods offered for sale. In this case the per-period level of consumption (C^p) is $C^p = \sqrt{(100 - y)x} + (y - x)/2$ where the term $(y - x)/2$ is the value of the money balances exchanged for consumption goods at the end of the experiment

(considering the convention regarding valuation of remaining money balances). Optimizing consumption with respect to x and y leads to the condition $x + y = 100$. Hence, a strategy with $x = 50$ and $y = 50$ is just as good as one with $x = 0$ and $y = 100$, that is, a strategy where all endowments are sold and cash is accumulated to be exchanged for goods in the final period of the experiment.

12. The experiment was programmed and conducted with the software z-Tree (see Fischbacher, 1999).

13. The time trend is statistically significant and the estimates show a significant downward trend during each run. One way to explain this trend is by way of a learning and adjustment process over the course of each run.

14. It fits this picture that there is no significant increase in output in the two economies after the increase in the money supply.

APPENDIX 11.1 INSTRUCTIONS FOR THE EXPERIMENT (TRANSLATED FROM GERMAN)

This experiment studies the use of money in economic transactions. The experimental economy in which you will become active is a monetary economy. As in economic reality you pay money for the purchase of goods and you receive money for the sale of goods. Hence, in the experiment you will not be allowed to buy goods directly with other goods. At the beginning of the experiment you will receive an endowment of money (100 units).

There are two goods in this economy (good A and good B) and two markets, one for either of these goods. In one of these markets you will act as a supplier of the good and in the other market you will act as a purchaser of the good. If the heading of your instruction sheet says you are an A-type this means that in every period of the experiment you will receive a specific amount of goods of type A but no B goods. In turn if you are labelled a B-type you will receive B goods as an endowment every period but no A goods. Both types of agents in this economy (A-types and B-types) are interested in acquiring goods that are not included in their endowment. The reason for this is that every participant in this economy produces a consumption good from A and B goods. The production relation that describes the input–output relation is $C = \sqrt{AB}$. Figure A11.1 shows the level of consumption output rounded to integer numbers as a function of inputs. Note that without the purchase of the other good your consumption output in any period is zero. Your aim is to maximize your cumulated consumption output over all market periods. For every unit of the consumption good that you produce you will earn 1 euro cent. The purchase and the sale of goods are realized for money in anonymous markets. This means you are offering money for the purchase of the good that is not in your endowment and you receive money for the good that you offer for sale. Except for the distinction of A-types and B-types, at the beginning of the experiment all participants have the same quantitative endowments.

Market Functioning

You have one variable for controlling your purchasing and selling behaviour, respectively:

a) For the good that is not in your endowment: Here, you set the sum of money that you are willing to offer for this type of good in a specific period.

Figure 11.A1   Production function for the consumption good

b)   For the good that is in your endowment: Here, you set the number of goods that you are willing to offer for sale in a specific period.

When all market participants have made their choices the market equilibrium price is determined as follows (these prices are derived under the assumption that your demand is isoelastic of degree one; this means that the quantity of goods demanded by you is equal to the ratio of money offered to the market price of the good):

$$P^A = \frac{\text{total of money units offered by purchasers of good } A}{\text{total quantity of goods } A \text{ offered for sale}}$$

$$P^B = \frac{\text{total of money units offered by purchasers of good } B}{\text{total quantity of goods } B \text{ offered for sale}}$$

The price of the good purchased thus set determines how many units of this good a purchaser buys: it is the quantity of money offered divided by this price. In the course of the market transactions that follow, A-types receive B-goods and B-types receive A-goods. Parallel to this flow of goods there is a flow of money: each market participant has an inflow of money equal to the value of his sales and an outflow of money equal to the value of his purchases. This means that depending on the individual decisions and the market price determined a market participant can have more or less money when all transactions of a period have been settled.

At the end of the experiment your final money balances are valued. You will receive at the average price of the last market period an equal number of A-goods and B-goods which go directly into the production of consumption goods. Accordingly, the value of your remaining money balances expressed in consumption good is the following:

$$\text{Value of your remaining money at the end of the experiment} = \frac{\text{remaining money balances}}{\text{price of good } B + \text{price of good } A}$$

The Course of the Experiment

The experiment consists of two runs of 20 periods each. At the beginning of each of these runs the money balances are set to 100 units. There is a trial phase of three periods before we start with the actual experiment. The outcome of the trial phase is of no relevance for your financial pay-off in terms of euro cents. For each period you will be given 150 seconds of time to make your entries. If you have not entered any data by the end of this time limit the experiment continues on the assumption that you want to repeat the entries from the previous period.

References

Akerlof, G.A. (1970), 'The market for "lemons": quality uncertainty and the market mechanism', *Quarterly Journal of Economics*, **84** (3), 488–500.

Allais, M. (1953), 'Le comportement de l'homme rationnel devant le risque: critique des postulats et axiomes de l'école américaine', *Econometrica*, **21**, 503–46.

Alpern, S. and D.J. Reyniers (2002), 'Spatial dispersion as a dynamic coordination problem', *Theory and Decision*, **53** (1), 29–59.

Amemiya, T. (1994), *Introduction to Statistics and Econometrics*, Cambridge, MA: Harvard University Press.

Antweiler, W. and M.Z. Frank (2004), 'Is all that talk just noise? The information content of internet stock message boards', *Journal of Finance*, **59** (3), 1259–94.

Armstrong, J.S. (2001), *Principles of Forecasting: A Handbook for Researchers and Practitioners*, Boston, MA: Kluwer Academic Press.

Arnett, J.J. (2000), 'Optimistic bias in adolescent and adult smokers and nonsmokers', *Addictive Behaviors*, **25** (4), 625–36.

Arrow, K.J. (1953), 'The role of securities in the optimal allocation of risk-bearing', *Econometrie*, as translated and reprinted in 1964, *Review of Economic Studies*, **31** (2), 91–6.

Arthur, W.B. (1991), 'Designing economic agents that act like human agents: a behavioral approach to bounded rationality', *American Economic Review*, **81** (2), 353–9.

Barberis, N., A. Shleifer and R. Vishny (1998), 'A model of investor sentiment', *Journal of Financial Economics*, **49** (3), 307–43.

Barsalou, L.W. (1992), *Cognitive Psychology: An Overview for Cognitive Scientists*, Hillsdale, NJ: Lawrence Erlbaum.

Battalio, R., L. Samuelson and J. Van Huyck (2001), 'Optimization incentives and coordination failure in laboratory stag hunt games', *Econometrica*, **69** (3), 749–64.

Baumol, W.J. (1952), 'The transactions demand for cash: an inventory theoretic approach', *Quarterly Journal of Economics*, **66** (4), 545–56.

Begg, D.K.H. (1982), *The Rational Expectations Revolution in Macroeconomics*, Oxford: Philip Allen.

Bernoulli, D. [1738] (1954), 'Exposition of a new theory on the measurement of risk', *Commentarii Academiae Scientiarum Imperialis Petropolitanae*, translated in, *Econometrica*, **22** (1), 23–36.

Besanko, D., D. Dranoce and M. Shanley (2000), *Economics of Strategy*, New York: John Wiley & Sons.

Blanchard, O.J. and S. Fischer (1989), *Lectures on Macroeconomics*, Cambridge, MA: MIT Press.

Bloomfield, R. and J. Hales (2002), 'Predicting the next step of a random walk: experimental evidence of regime-shifting beliefs', *Journal of Financial Economics*, **65**, 397–414.

Bolle, F. (1988a), 'Testing for rational expectations in experimental predictions', in S. Maital (ed.), *Behavioral Economics*, Amsterdam: North-Holland.

Bolle, F. (1988b), 'Learning to make good predictions for the following value in a time series', in W. Albers, R. Selten and R. Tietz (eds), *Modeling Bounded Rational Behavior in Experimental Games and Markets*, Springer Lecture Notes 314.

Bolton, P. and M. Dewatripont (2005), *Contract Theory*, Cambridge, MA: MIT Press.

Bomfim, A.N. (2001), 'Heterogeneous forecasts and aggregate dynamics', *Journal of Monetary Economics*, **47** (1), 145–61.

Bonham, C. and R. Cohen (1995), 'Testing the rationality of price forecasts: comment', *American Economic Review*, **85** (1), 284–9.

Bowman, M.J. (1958), 'Introduction', in M.J. Bowman (ed.), *Expectations, Uncertainty, and Business Behavior*, New York: Social Science Research Council.

Branch, W.A. (2004), 'The theory of rationally heterogeneous expectations: evidence from survey data on inflation expectations', *Economic Journal*, **114** (497), 592–621.

Brehmer, B. (1980), 'In one word: not from experience', *Acta Psychologica*, **45**, 223–41.

Brock, W.A. (1975), 'A simple perfect foresight monetary model', *Journal of Monetary Economics*, **1** (2), 133–50.

Brock, W.A. and C.H. Hommes (1997), 'A rational route to randomness', *Econometrica*, **65** (5), 1059–95.

Brown, K.C. and D.J. Brown (1984), 'Heterogenous expectations and farmland prices', *American Journal of Agricultural Economics*, **66** (2), 164–9.

Bryant, J. (1983), 'A simple rational expectations Keynes-type model', *Quarterly Journal of Economics*, **98** (3), 525–8.

Buchanan, N.S. (1939), 'A reconsideration of the cobweb theorem', *Journal of Political Economy*, **47** (1), 67–81.

Busemeyer, J.R. and A. Rapoport (1988), 'Psychological models of deferred decision making', *Journal of Mathematical Psychology*, **32**, 1–44.

Byamugisha, F. and W. Zakout (2000), 'World Bank support for land-related projects in developing countries: experiences and implications for international cooperation', mimeo, World Bank.

Camerer, C.F. (1987), 'Do biases in probability judgment matter in markets? Experimental evidence', *American Economic Review*, **77** (5), 981–97.

Caplin, A. and J. Leahy (2003), 'Behavioral Policy', in I. Brocas and J.D. Carrillo (eds), *The Psychology of Economic Decisions*, New York: Oxford University Press.

Caplin, A. and J. Leahy (2004), 'The supply of information by a concerned expert', *Economic Journal*, **114** (497), 487–505.

Caskey, J. (1985), 'Modeling the formation of price expectations: a Bayesian approach', *American Economic Review*, **75** (4), 768–76.

Champsaur, P. and J.-C. Milleron (1983), *Advanced Exercises in Microeconomics*, Cambridge, MA: Harvard University Press.

Cheung, Y.-W., M. Chinn and A. Pascual (2005), 'Empirical exchange rate models of the nineties: are any fit to survive?' *Journal of International Money and Finance*, **24** (7), 1150–75.

Chow, G.C. (1989), 'Rational versus adaptive expectations in present value models', *Review of Economics and Statistics*, **71** (3), 376–84.

Ciccone, S.J. (2005), 'Trends in analyst earnings forecast properties', *International Review of Financial Analysis*, **14** (1), 1–22.

Clower, R.W. (1967), 'A reconsideration of the microfoundations of monetary theory', *Western Economic Journal*, **6** (1), 1–9.

Cohen, R.B., C. Polk and T. Vuolteenaho (2005), 'Money illusion in the stock market: the Modigliani-Cohn hypothesis', *Quarterly Journal of Economics*, **120** (2), 639–68.

Conlisk, J. (1996), 'Why bounded rationality?' *Journal of Economic Literature*, **34** (2), 669–700.

Connolly, T. and B.K. Thorn (1987), 'Predecisional information acquisition: effects of task variables on suboptimal research strategies', *Organizational Behavior and Human Decision Processes*, **39**, 397–416.

Cooper, A.C., T.B. Folta and C. Woo (2001), 'Entrepreneurial information search', *Journal of Business Venturing*, **10** (2), 107–20.

Cooper, D.J., S. Garvin and J.H. Kagel (1997), 'Adaptive learning vs. equilibrium refinements in an entry limit pricing game', *Economic Journal*, **107** (442), 553–75.

Cooper, R.W. (1999), *Coordination Games: Complementarities and Macroeconomics*, Cambridge: Cambridge University Press.

Cooper, W.W. and H.A. Simon (1955), 'Economic expectations and plans of firms in relation to short-term forecasting', Comment by Modigliani and Sauerlender, *Studies in Income and Wealth*, **17**, 352–9.

Cothren, R. (1983), 'Job search and implicit contracts', *Journal of Political Economy*, **91** (3), 494–504.

Cox, J.C. and D.M. Grether (1996), 'The preference reversal phenomenon: response mode, markets and incentives', *Economic Theory*, **7** (3), 381–405.

Crawford, V.P. (1991), 'An "evolutionary" interpretation of Van Huyck, Battalio and Beil's experimental results on coordination', *Games and Economic Behavior*, **3** (1), 25–59.

Crawford, V.P. and H. Haller (1990), 'Learning how to cooperate: optimal play in repeated coordination games', *Econometrica*, **58** (3), 571–95.

Cuthbertson, K. (1996), *Quantitative Financial Economics: Stocks, Bonds and Foreign Exchange*, Chichester: John Wiley & Sons.

Debreu, G. (1959), *Theory of Value: An Axiomatic Analysis of Economic Equilibrium*, New Haven, CT: Yale University Press.

De Bondt, W. (1993), 'Betting on trends: intuitive forecasts of financial risk and return', *International Journal of Forecasting*, **9**, 355–71.

De Bondt, W. and R.H. Thaler (1985), 'Does the stock market overreact?' *Journal of Finance*, **40**, 793–805.

De Grauwe, P. and H. Dewachter (1993), 'A chaotic model of the exchange rate: the role of fundamentalists and chartists', *Open Economics Review*, **4**, 351–79.

De Long, J.B., A. Shleifer, L.H. Summers and R.J. Waldmann (1990), 'Noise trader risk in financial markets', *Journal of Political Economy*, **98** (4), 703–38.

Dixit, A.K. and R.S. Pindyck (1994), *Investment Under Uncertainty*, Princeton, NJ: Princeton University Press.

Dominitz, J. (1998), 'Earnings expectations, revisions, and realizations', *Review of Economics and Statistics*, **80** (3), 374–88.

Dominitz, J. and C.F. Manski (2006), 'Measuring pension-benefit expectations probabilistically', *Labour*, **20** (2), 201–36.

Dornbusch, R. and J.A. Frenkel (1973), 'Inflation and growth: alternative approaches', *Journal of Money, Credit, and Banking*, Part I, **5** (1), 141–56.

Duffy, J. (1998), 'Monetary theory in the laboratory', *Federal Reserve Bank of St Louis, Review*, **80** (5), 9–26.

Duffy, J. and E. O'N. Fisher (2005), 'Sunspots in the laboratory', *American Economic Review*, **95** (3), 510–29.

Dwyer, G.P. Jr., A.W. Williams, R.C. Battalio and T.I. Mason (1993), 'Tests of rational expectations in a stark setting', *Economic Journal*, **103** (418), 586–601.

Eeckhoudt, L., C. Gollier and H. Schlesinger (2005), *Economic and Financial Decisions under Risk*, Princeton, NJ: Princeton University Press.

Eggleton, I.R.C. (1982), 'Intuitive time-series extrapolation', *Journal of Accounting Research*, **20**, 68–102.

Erev, I. and A.E. Roth (1998), 'Predicting how people play games: reinforcement learning in experimental games with unique, mixed strategy equilibria', *American Economic Review*, **88** (4), 848–81.

Evans, G.W. and S. Honkapohja (2001), *Learning and Expectations in Macroeconomics*, Princeton, NJ: Princeton University Press.

Evans, M.D.D. and R.K. Lyons (2005), 'Meese-Rogoff redux: micro-based exchange-rate forecasting', *American Economic Review*, **95** (2), 405–14.

Eysenck, M.W. and N. Derakshan (1997), 'Cognitive biases for future negative events as a function of trait anxiety and social desirability', *Personality and Individual Differences*, **22**, 597–605.

Ezekiel, M. (1938), 'The cobweb theorem', *Quarterly Journal of Economics*, **52** (2), 255–80.

Fehr, E. and J.-R. Tyran (2001), 'Does money illusion matter?' *American Economic Review*, **91** (5), 1239–62.

Feldman, J. (1963), 'Simulation of behavior in the binary choice experiment', in E.A. Feigenbaum and J. Feldman (eds), *Computers and Thought*, New York: McGraw-Hill.

Figlewski, S. and P. Wachtel (1981), 'The formation of inflationary expectations', *Review of Economics and Statistics*, **63** (1), 1–10.

Fischbacher, U. (1999), 'Z-Tree: Zurich toolbox for readymade economic experiments', IEW Working Paper 21, University of Zurich.

Fisher, F.M. (1962), *A Priori Information and Time Series Analysis: Essays in Economic Theory and Measurement*, Amsterdam: North-Holland.

Frankel, J.A. and K.A. Froot (1986), 'Understanding the dollar in the eighties: the expectations of chartists and fundamentalists', *Economic Record*, **62** (Supplementary Issue), 24–38.

Frankel, J.A. and K.A. Froot (1990), 'Chartists, fundamentalists, and trading in the foreign exchange market', *American Economic Review*, **80** (2), 181–5.

Frantz, R. (2003), 'Herbert Simon: artificial intelligence as a framework for understanding intuition', *Journal of Economic Psychology*, **24**, 265–77.

Friedman, M. (1953), *Essays in Positive Economics*, Chicago, IL: Chicago University Press.

Friedman, M. (1956), 'The quantity theory of money – a restatement', in M. Friedman (ed.), *Studies in the Quantity Theory of Money*, Chicago, IL: University of Chicago Press.

Frieze, I.H., J.E. Parsons, P.B. Johnson, D.N. Ruble and G.L. Zellman (1978), *Women and Sex Roles*, New York: Norton.

Gabrynowicz, J.I. (2003), 'Licensing and the Landsat story: law and policy', presentation to the National Research Council Committee on Licensing Geographic Data and Services, mimeo, National Remote Sensing and Space Law Center, University of Mississippi School of Law.

Gardes, F. and G. Prat (2000), *Price Expectations in Goods and Financial Markets*, Cheltenham, UK and Northampton, MA, USA: Edward Elgar.

Gilboa, I. and D. Schmeidler (1995), 'Case-based decision theory', *Quarterly Journal of Economics*, **110** (3), 605–39.

Goodhart, C. (1990), 'News and the foreign exchange market', LSE Financial Market Group Discussion Paper No. 71.

Guesnerie, R. (2001), *Assessing Rational Expectations: Sunspot Multiplicity and Economic Fluctuations*, Cambridge, MA: MIT Press.

Haltiwanger, J.C. and M. Waldman (1989), 'Limited rationality and strategic complements: the implications for macroeconomics', *Quarterly Journal of Economics*, **104** (3), 463–83.

Hamouda, O.F. and J.C.R. Rowley (1996), *Probability in Economics*, London: Routledge.

Hays, P.L. (2002), 'What is spacepower and does it constitute a revolution in military affairs?' *Journal of Military and Strategic Studies*, **5** (1), 1–28.

Heine, S.J. and D.R. Lehman (1995), 'Cultural variation in unrealistic optimism: does the west feel more invulnerable than the east?' *Journal of Personality and Social Psychology*, **68**, 595–607.

Herrnstein, R.J. and D. Prelec (1991), 'Melioration: a theory of distributed choice', *Journal of Economic Perspectives*, **5** (3), 137–56.

Hey, J.D. (1984), 'The economics of optimism and pessimism', *Kyklos*, **37** (2), 181–205.

Hey, J.D. (1994), 'Expectations formation: rational or adaptive or . . .?' *Journal of Economic Behavior and Organization*, **25** (3), 329–49.

Hey, J.D. (2003), *Intermediate Microeconomics: People are Different*, London: McGraw-Hill.

Hicks, J. (1969), *A Theory of Economic History*, Oxford: Oxford University Press.

Hicks, J. (1989), *A Market Theory of Money*, Oxford: Oxford University Press.

Hill, J. and B. Schütt (2000), 'Mapping complex patterns of erosion and stability in dry mediterranean ecosystems', *Remote Sensing of Environment*, **74** (3), 557–69.

Hirshleifer, D. (2001), 'Investor psychology and asset pricing', *Journal of Finance*, **56** (4), 1533–97.

Hirshleifer, J. and J.G. Riley (1992), *The Analytics of Uncertainty and Information*, Cambridge: Cambridge University Press.

Holden, K., D.A. Peel and J.L. Thompson (1985), *Expectations: Theory and Evidence*, Basingstoke: Macmillan.

Hong, H. and J.C. Stein (2003), 'Simple forecasts and paradigm shifts', National Bureau of Economic Research Working Paper, No. 10013.

Hopper, G.P. (1997), 'What determines the exchange rate: economic factors or market sentiment?' *Federal Reserve Bank of Philadelphia Business Review*, September, 17–29.

Ito, T. (1990), 'Foreign exchange rate expectations: micro survey data', *American Economic Review*, **80** (3), 434–49.

Jeong, J. and G.S. Maddala (1991), 'Measurement errors and tests for rationality', *Journal of Business and Economic Statistics*, **9** (4), 431–9.

Jones, B. (2003), 'Bounded rationality and political science: lessons from public administration and public policy', *Journal of Public Administration Research and Theory*, **13** (4), 395–412.

Jones, M.R. (1971), 'From probability learning to sequential processing: a critical view', *Psychological Bulletin*, **76**, 153–85.

Kahneman, D. (2003), 'Maps of bounded rationality: psychology for behavioral economics', *American Economic Review*, **93** (5), 1449–75.

Kahneman, D. and A. Tversky (1979), 'Prospect theory: an analysis of decision under risk', *Econometrica*, **47** (2), 263–91.

Katona, G. (1946), 'Psychological analysis of business decisions and expectations', *American Economic Review*, **36** (1), 44–62.

Keane, M.P. and D.E. Runkle (1990), 'Testing the rationality of price forecasts: new evidence from panel data', *American Economic Review*, **80** (4), 714–35.

Kelly, M. (1997), 'Do noise traders influence stock prices?' *Journal of Money, Credit, and Banking*, **29** (3), 351–63.

Keynes, J.M. (1936), *The General Theory of Employment, Interest and Money*, London: Macmillan.

Kirman, A.P. (1992), 'Whom or what does the representative individual represent?' *Journal of Economic Perspectives*, **6** (2), 117–36.

Kiyotaki, N. and R. Wright (1989), 'On money as a medium of exchange', *Journal of Political Economy*, **97** (4), 927–54.

Kiyotaki, N. and R. Wright (1992), 'Acceptability, Means of Payment, and Media of Exchange', *The New Palgrave Dictionary of Money and Finance*, London: Macmillan.

Kmenta, J. (1971), *Elements of Econometrics*, New York: Macmillan.

Krugman, P.R., T. Persson and L.E.O. Svensson (1985), 'Inflation, interest rates, and welfare', *Quarterly Journal of Economics*, **100** (3), 677–95.

Laibson, D. (1997), 'Golden eggs and hyperbolic discounting', *Quarterly Journal of Economics*, **112** (2), 443–77.

Lee, K.C. (1994), 'Formation of price and cost inflation expectations in British manufacturing industries: a multi-sectoral analysis', *Economic Journal*, **104**, 372–85.

LeRoy, S.F. (2004), 'Rational exuberance', *Journal of Economic Literature*, **42** (3), 783–804.

Levine, D.I. (1993), 'Do corporate executives have rational expectations?' *Journal of Business*, **66** (2), 271–93.

Lo, A.W., H. Mamaysky and J. Wang (2000), 'Foundations of technical analysis: computational algorithms, statistical inference, and empirical implementation', *Journal of Finance*, **55** (4),1705–65.

Lovell, M.C. (1986), 'Tests of the rational expectations hypothesis', *American Economic Review*, **76** (1), 110–24.

Lucas, R. (1978), 'Asset pricing in an exchange economy', *Econometrica*, **46** (6), 1429–45.

Ludowicy, C., R. Schwaiberger and P. Leithold (2002), *Precision Farming: Handbuch für die Praxis*, Frankfurt am Main: DLG-Verlags-GmbH.

Lund, N. (2001), *Attention and Pattern Recognition*, London: Routledge.

Lundberg, S.J. and R. Startz (1983), 'Private discrimination and social intervention in competitive labor market', *American Economic Review*, **73** (3), 340–47.

Macauley, M.K. and M.A. Toman (1991), 'Providing earth observation data from space: economics and institutions', *American Economic Review*, **81** (2), 38–41.

Machina, M.J. (1989), 'Dynamic consistency and non-expected utility models of choice under uncertainty', *Journal of Economic Literature*, **27**, 1622–68.

Marimon, R. and S. Sunder (1993), 'Indeterminacy of equilibria in a hyper-inflationary world: experimental evidence', *Econometrica*, **61** (5), 1073–107.

Marimon, R. and S. Sunder (1994), 'Expectations and learning under alternative monetary regimes', *Economic Theory*, **4** (1), 131–62.

Marimon, R. and S. Sunder (1995), 'Does a constant money growth rule help stabilize inflation? Experimental evidence', *Carnegie Rochester Conference Series on Public Policy*, **43** (December), 111–56.

Markowitz, H. (1952), 'Portfolio selection', *Journal of Finance*, **7** (1), 77–91.

Markowitz, H. (1959), *Portfolio Selection: Efficient Diversification of Investments*, New York: John Wiley & Sons.

McCallum, B.T. (1989), *Monetary Economics: Theory and Policy*, New York: Macmillan.

McCallum, B.T. (2004), 'Consistent expectations, rational expectations, multiple-solution indeterminacies, and least-squares learnability', in

P. Minford (ed.), *Money Matters: Essays in Honour of Alan Walters*, Cheltenham, UK and Northampton, MA, USA: Edward Elgar.

McDonald, R. and D. Siegel (1986), 'The value of waiting to invest', *Quarterly Journal of Economics*, **101** (4), 707–28.

Meese, R. and K. Rogoff (1983), 'Empirical exchange rate models of the seventies', *Journal of International Economics*, **14** (1–2), 3–24.

Mirman, L.J., L. Samuelson and A. Urbano (1993), 'Monopoly experimentation', *International Economic Review*, **34** (3), 549–63.

Morris, S. and H.S. Shin (2000), 'Rethinking multiple equilibria in macroeconomic modeling', *NBER Macroeconomics Annual*, 139–61.

Muth, J.F. (1960), 'Optimal properties of exponentially weighted forecasts', *Journal of the American Statistical Association*, **55** (290), 299–306.

Muth, J.F. (1961), 'Rational expectations and the theory of price movements', *Econometrica*, **29** (3), 315–35.

National Research Council (1997), *Precision Agriculture in the 21st Century: Geospatial and Information Technologies in Crop Management*, Washington, DC: National Academy Press.

Nerlove, M. (1983), 'Expectations, plans, and realizations in theory and practice', *Econometrica*, **51** (5), 1251–80.

Nerlove, M. and I. Fornari (1998), 'Quasi-rational expectations, an alternative to fully rational expectations: an application to US beef cattle supply', *Journal of Econometrics*, **83** (1–2), 129–61.

Newell, B.R., T. Rakow, N.J. Weston and D.R. Shanks (2004), 'Search strategies in decision making: the success of "success"', *Journal of Behavioral Decision Making*, **17** (2), 117–37.

Niehans, J. (1978), *The Theory of Money*, Baltimore, MD: Johns Hopkins University Press.

Niehans, J. (1997), 'Adam Smith and the welfare cost of optimism', *History of Political Economy*, **29** (2), 185–200.

Nyhus, E.K. and P. Webley (2006), 'Discounting, self-control and saving', in M. Altman (ed.), *Handbook of Contemporary Behavioral Economics: Foundations and Developments*, Armonk, NY: M.E. Sharpe Publishers.

Obstfeld, M. (1984), 'Multiple stable equilibria in an optimizing perfect-foresight model', *Econometrica*, **52** (1), 223–8.

Ochs, J. (1995), 'Coordination games', in J.H. Kagel and A.E. Roth (eds), *The Handbook of Experimental Economics*, Princeton, NJ: Princeton University Press.

Office of Technology Assessment (1984), *Remote Sensing and the Private Sector: Issues for Discussion – A Technical Memorandum*, Washington, DC: US Congress.

Patinkin, D. (1949), 'The indeterminacy of absolute prices in classical economic theory', *Econometrica*, **17** (1), 1–27.

Patinkin, D. (1950–51), 'A reconsideration of the general equilibrium theory of money', *Review of Economic Studies*, **18** (1), 42–61.

Pesaran, M.H. (1987), *The Limits to Rational Expectations*, New York: Basil Blackwell.

Pigou, A.C. (1927), *Industrial Fluctuations*, London: Macmillan.

Pingle, M. (1992), 'Costly optimization: an experiment', *Journal of Economic Behavior and Organization*, **17** (1), 3–30.

Pingle, M. (2006), 'Deliberation cost as a foundation for behavioral economics', in M. Altman (ed.), *Handbook of Contemporary Behavioral Economics: Foundations and Developments*, Armonk, NY: M.E. Sharpe Publishers.

Pingle, M. and R.H. Day (1996), 'Modes of economizing behavior: experimental evidence', *Journal of Economic Behavior and Organization*, **29** (2), 191–209.

Plott, C.R. (1987), 'Rational Choice in Experimental Markets', in R. Hogarth and M. Reder (eds), *Rational Choice: The Contrast between Economics and Psychology*, Chicago, IL: University of Chicago Press.

Plott, C.R. and S. Sunder (1988), 'Rational expectations and the aggregation of diverse information in laboratory security markets', *Econometrica*, **56** (5), 1085–118.

Pope, R.D. (1981), 'Supply response and the dispersion of price expectations', *American Journal of Agricultural Economics*, **63** (1), 161–3.

Porter, D.P. and V.L. Smith (2003), 'Stock market bubbles in the laboratory', *Journal of Behavioral Finance*, **4** (1), 7–20.

Posner, M.I. (1989), *The Foundations of Cognitive Science*, Cambridge, MA: MIT Press.

Pötzelberger, K. and L. Sögner (2004), 'Sample autocorrelation learning in a capital market model', *Journal of Economic Behavior and Organization*, **53** (2), 215–36.

Pruitt, S.W. and L.J. Gitman (1987), 'Capital budgeting forecast biases: evidence from the Fortune 500', *Financial Management*, **16**, 46–51; reprinted in D.J. Lamdin (ed.) (1996), *Managerial Economics Reader*, Oxford: Blackwell.

Puccetti, R. (1974), 'Pattern recognition in computers and the human brain: with special application to chess playing machines', *British Journal for the Philosophy of Science*, **25** (2), 137–54.

Rabin, M. (1998), 'Psychology and economics', *Journal of Economic Literature*, **36** (1), 11–46.

Radner, R. (1982), 'Equilibrium under uncertainty', in K.J. Arrow and M.D. Intriligator (eds), *Handbook of Mathematical Economics*, Vol. 2, Amsterdam: North-Holland.

Radner, R. (2000), 'Costly and bounded rationality in individual and team decision-making', *Industrial and Corporate Change*, **9** (4), 623–58.

Rajeev, G. and J.C. Fox (2002), *Judgments, Decisions and Public Policy*, Cambridge: Cambridge University Press.

Richardson, G.B. (1959), 'Equilibrium, expectations and information', *Economic Journal* **69**, (274), 223–37.

Rötheli, T.F. (1996), 'Price and output effects of heterogeneous expectations', *Swiss Journal of Economics and Statistics*, **132** (2), 207–22.

Rötheli, T.F. (1998), 'Pattern recognition and procedurally rational expectations', *Journal of Economic Behavior and Organization*, **37** (1), 71–90.

Rötheli, T.F. (1999), 'Selling prices and profits: what survey data tell about firms' rationality', *Managerial and Decision Economics*, **20** (6), 319–25.

Rötheli, T.F. (2001), 'Acquisition of costly information: an experimental study', *Journal of Economic Behavior and Organization*, **46** (2), 193–208.

Rötheli, T.F. (2005), 'The illusion of over-optimism in survey data: the case of manufacturers' selling prices', *Journal of Socio-Economics*, **34** (2), 151–9.

Rötheli, T.F. (2006), 'Elements of behavioral monetary economics', in M. Altman (ed.), *Handbook of Contemporary Behavioral Economics: Foundations and Developments*, Armonk, NY: M.E. Sharpe Publishers.

Rousseau, J.-J. [1755] (1979), *Discours sur l'origine et les fondements de l'inégalité parmi les hommes*, Paris: Edition Sociales.

Rumelhart, D.E., J.L. McClelland and the PDP Research Group (1986), *Parallel Distributed Processing: Explorations in the Microstructure of Cognition, Volume 1: Foundations*, Cambridge, MA: MIT Press.

Saatchi, S.S., J.V. Soares and D.S. Alves (1997), 'Mapping deforestation and land use in amazon rainforest by using SIR-C imagery', *Remote Sensing of Environment*, **59** (2), 191–202.

Salanie, B. (1997), *The Economics of Contracts: A Primer*, Cambridge, MA: MIT Press.

Samuelson, P.A. (1958), 'An exact consumption-loan model of interest with or without the social contrivance of money', *Journal of Political Economy*, **66** (6), 467–82.

Sannier, C.A.D., J.C. Taylor and W. Du Plessis (2002), 'Real-time monitoring of vegetation biomass with NOAA-AVHRR in Etosha National Park, Namibia, for fire risk assessment', *International Journal of Remote Sensing*, **23** (1), 71–89.

Sargent, T.J. and N. Wallace (1975), ' "Rational" expectations, the optimal monetary instrument, and the optimal money supply rule', *Journal of Political Economy*, **83** (2), 241–54.

Sarle, C.F. (1925), 'The forecasting of the price of hogs', *American Economic Review*, **15** (3, Supplement), 1–22.

Schelling, T.C. (1960), *The Strategy of Conflict*, Cambridge, MA: Harvard University Press.

Schmalensee, R. (1976), 'An experimental study of expectation formation', *Econometrica*, **44** (1), 17–41.

Schoemaker, P.J.H. (1982), 'The expected utility model: its variants, purposes, evidence and limitations', *Journal of Economic Literature*, **20** (2), 529–63.

Scitovsky, T. (1954), 'Two concepts of external economies', *Journal of Political Economy*, **62** (2), 143–51.

Selten, R. (1998), 'Features of experimentally observed bounded rationality', *European Economic Review*, **42** (3–5), 413–36.

Shanks, D.R. (1995), 'Is human learning rational?' *Quarterly Journal of Experimental Psychology*, **48A**, 257–79.

Shefrin, H. (2005), *A Behavioral Approach to Asset Pricing*, Burlington, MA: Elsevier Academic Press.

Shiller, R.J. (1981), 'Do stock prices move too much to be justified by subsequent changes in dividends?' *American Economic Review*, **71** (3), 421–36.

Shiller, R.J. (2001), *Irrational Exuberance*, New York: Princeton University Press.

Shleifer, A. and Summers, L.H. (1990), 'The noise trader approach to finance', *Journal of Economic Perspectives*, **4** (2), 19–33.

Shubik, M. (1990), 'A game theoretic approach to the theory of money and financial institutions', in B.M. Friedman and F.H. Hahn (eds), *Handbook of Monetary Economics*, Vol. I, Amsterdam: Elsevier Science Publishers.

Simon, H.A. (1959), 'Theories of decision-making in economics and behavioral science', *American Economic Review*, **49** (3), 253–83.

Simon, H.A. (1972), 'Theories of bounded rationality', in C.B. McGuire and R. Radner (eds), *Decision and Organization: A Volume in Honor of Jacob Marschak*, Amsterdam: North-Holland.

Simon, H.A. (1983), *Models of Bounded Rationality: Economic Analysis and Public Policy*, Vol. 1, Cambridge, MA: MIT Press.

Skyrms, B. (2003), *The Stag Hunt and the Evolution of Social Structure*, Cambridge: Cambridge University Press.

Smith, V.L., G.L. Suchanek and A.W. Williams (1988), 'Bubbles, crashes, and endogenous expectations in experimental spot asset markets', *Econometrica*, **56** (5), 1119–51.

Smyth, D.J. (1992), 'Measurement errors in survey forecasts of expected inflation and the rationality of inflation expectations', *Journal of Macroeconomics*, **14**, 439–48.

Sugden, R. (1995), 'A theory of focal points', *Economic Journal*, **105** (430), 533–50.

Thaler, R.H. (1994), 'Savings policies', *American Economic Review*, **84** (2), 186–92.

Timmermann, A. (1994), 'Can agents learn to form rational expectations? Some results on convergence and stability of learning in the UK stock market', *Economic Journal*, **104** (425), 777–97.

Tobin, J. (1958), 'Liquidity preference as behavior toward risk', *Review of Economic Studies*, **25** (2), 65–86.

Todd, P.M. (2001), 'Heuristics for decision and choice', in N.J. Smelser and P.B. Baltes (eds), *International Encyclopedia of the Social and Behavioral Sciences*, Amsterdam: Elsevier.

Turnovsky, S.J. (1983), 'The determination of spot and futures prices with storable commodities', *Econometrica*, **51** (5), 1363–88.

Turnovsky, S.J. (2000), *Methods of Macroeconomic Dynamics*, Cambridge, MA: MIT Press.

Tversky, A. and D. Kahneman (1992), 'Advances in prospect theory: cumulative representation of uncertainty', *Journal of Risk and Uncertainty*, **5** (4), 297–323.

Tyebjee, T.T. (1987), 'Behavioral biases in new product forecasting', *International Journal of Forecasting*, **3**, 393–404.

Usher, J.M. and D.D. Truax (2001), 'Exploration of remote sensing applicability within transportation', mimeo, Mississippi State University Remote Sensing Technology Center (RSTC).

Van Huyck, J.B., R.C. Battalio and R.O. Beil (1990), 'Tacit coordination games, strategic uncertainty, and coordination failure', *American Economic Review*, **80** (1), 234–48.

Van Huyck, J.B., R.C. Battalio and R.O. Beil (1991), 'Strategic uncertainty, equilibrium selection, and coordination failure in average opinion games', *Quarterly Journal of Economics*, **106** (3), 885–910.

Von Neumann, J. and O. Morgenstern (1947), *Theory of Games and Economic Behavior*, (2nd edn), Princeton, NJ: Princeton University Press.

Wald, A. (1950), *Statistical Decision Functions*, New York: John Wiley & Sons.

Waldman, M. (1994), 'Systematic errors and the theory of natural selection', *American Economic Review*, **84** (3), 482–97.

Wenzelburger, J. (2004), 'Learning to predict rationally when beliefs are heterogeneous', *Journal of Economic Dynamics and Control*, **28** (10), 2075–104.

Wicksell, K. (1898), *Geldzins und Güterpeise*, Jena: G. Fischer.

Williams, A.W. (1987), 'The formation of price forecasts in experimental markets', *Journal of Money, Credit and Banking*, **19** (1), 1–18.

Wright, G. and P. Ayton (eds) (1994), *Subjective Probability*, New York: John Wiley & Sons.

Zeckhauser, R., J. Patel and D. Hendricks (1991), 'Nonrational actors and financial market behavior', *Theory and Decision*, **31**, 257–87.

Zellner, A. (1986), 'Biased predictors, rationality and the evaluation of forecasts', *Economic Letters*, **21** (1), 45–8.

Index